D0114335

THE
YOKE
OF CHRIST
and other
sermons

Other books by Elton Trueblood

Philosophy of Religion
Declaration of Freedom
The Recovery of Family Life
Your Other Vocation
The Life We Prize
Signs of Hope In a Century of Despair
The Common Ventures of Life
Alternative to Futility
Foundations for Reconstruction
Doctor Johnson's Prayers
The Predicament of Modern Man
The Logic of Belief

THE
YOKE
OF CHRIST

and other
sermons

BY
ELTON
TRUEBLOOD

HARPER &
BROTHERS
NEW YORK

THE YOKE OF CHRIST

Copyright © 1958 by David Elton Trueblood

FIRST EDITION

I-H

Library of Congress catalog card number: 58-10364

TO
VIRGINIA

who would not let the idea rest

CONTENTS

PREFACE   9

The Yoke of Christ   11

The Salt of the Earth   22

The Gates of Hell   31

The Keys of the Kingdom   41

Conversion Within the Church   50

Called to be Saints   60

The Courage to Care   70

The Violence of the Kingdom   81

The Transcendence of Prudence   90

The Necessity of Witness   99

The Problem of the Crowd   108

The Emerging Order   118

The Discipline of Discipleship   128

The Abolition of the Laity   138

The Ministry of Daily Work   150

A Faith for Scientists   160

The Power of Small Fellowships   172

The Home as a Foretaste of the Kingdom   182

PREFACE

The difference between a sermon and a lecture is fundamentally a difference of aim. Whereas a lecture has a subject, a sermon has an object. Though a lecture may be devoted to any subject, including religion, the existence of such a subject is not sufficient to change a lecture into a sermon. It is not a sermon unless it is given in the hope of making a practical difference in the lives of the people who listen. The sermon is akin to art, in Aristotle's sense, in that it represents "a productive state of mind." It seeks to produce, to effect change, to alter the course of events. Always, in one way or another, the purpose is new life.

It is because the chapters in this volume have been written with such an object in view that they are called sermons. All are intended to influence decision in the critical period in which we live. This volume is concerned, therefore, not primarily with philosophy and not primarily with theology, but with the tremendous difference which the Christian gospel can make when it becomes relevant to the daily lives of ordinary men and women. This theme provides the reason for the particular selection of addresses and for the order in which they appear.

In the development of the central theme, an effort has been made to keep in mind both the reasons of the head and the reasons of the heart. This is because Christianity is not best served by a sharp division of labor between those who are called scholars and those whose lives are devoted to practical matters. The Christian scholar is a better scholar if he accepts some practical responsibilities in Christian work, and the practical worker is more likely to perform his ministry adequately if he is also concerned with some intellectual inquiry.

Nearly all of these addresses are now being published for the first time after having been delivered, with minor local variations, in a number of different settings. The only exceptions are three, as follows: "Conversion within the Church" has appeared in *The Christian Herald* for June, 1958, with the title, "America's Biggest Unevangelized Field: The Church," and is now used again, by permission, with some alterations. Part of the twelfth sermon appeared originally in *Presbyterian Life* in April, 1950. A few paragraphs of the third and of the eighteenth sermons appeared earlier in "Finding God in the Redemptive Fellowship," published as a pamphlet by the Upper Room, of Nashville, Tennessee. "A Faith for Scientists" was written specifically in response to the invitation of the American Association for the Advancement of Science, but it has not been previously published.

Several of these addresses have been given in college and university chapels, some in local churches of various denominations, and others in conferences. The wide use of this material, in oral form, means that all of it has profited by the reactions of a variety of hearers, thus being subject, before publication, to a truly experimental test. The purpose of publication now is to enlarge the fellowship of shared ideas.

E.T.

EARLHAM COLLEGE
JUNE, 1958

10

THE YOKE OF CHRIST

Come to me, all who labor and are heavy-laden, and I will give you rest. Take my yoke upon you and learn from me; for I am gentle and lowly in heart, and you will find rest for your souls. For my yoke is easy and my burden is light. MATTHEW 11:29, 30.[1]

It is not easy to be a human being. Human life carries with it marvelous possibilities of joy, but there are, at the same time, untold ways in which it can go wrong. Even after we have learned all that we can of the literature of tragedy, we have but an imperfect sense of the sorrow and frustrations which occur in countless lives. The harm that comes from the ravages of disease is terrible, but the harm that comes from the hatred and ignorance of other men is even more terrible. Often we are shocked when we realize that the persons who are near us are suffering in some serious way without our consciousness either of the fact or of the degree of the seriousness. My neighbor kills himself, and I have to admit that I did not even realize that he was particularly troubled. I am ashamed that I did not know, and I wonder why I did not suspect that he was in distress. Would I have known if I had been more sensitive to his need and less occupied with my own troubles? It is sobering to realize that the person next to

[1] Scripture references are from the Revised Standard Version, unless otherwise noted.

you on the train, or even in a congregation, may be struggling with problems that seem insoluble. We read in the newspapers of the harm that comes to individuals, but we forget about it because the story appears only one day. The awful fact, however, is that the tragedy does not end with the disappearance of the newspaper story. Many of the people of whom we have read, but soon forget, are living out the rest of their days in quiet desperation. The maimed are still maimed.

The universality of human sorrow and need is one of the reasons for the great attractiveness of the words of Jesus which appear at the end of the eleventh chapter of Matthew. When Jesus says, "Come unto me, all ye who labor and are_ heavy laden," He is really speaking to all. Every life has some serious burdens and most persons have, at one time or another, been overworked. We have tasks to perform, responsibilities to bear, problems to solve, promises to keep. Millions on the earth are bound so firmly to the economic wheel, with children to support, debts to pay, and living costs to meet, that they have no prospect of freedom as long as they live. The truth is that most people are poor! There is always the possibility of great joy in work accomplished, but for millions, work is nothing but a series of painful burdens. Great numbers, even in advanced civilizations, admit freely that they would stop work in a minute, were it not for the necessity of earning the means of survival for themselves and for those dependent upon them. Christ's words strike a responsive note because, for the most part, life is hard. Almost everyone feels that the words of this particular passage are addressed directly to him.

Another reason for the attractiveness of these sentences is the fact that they include Christ's clearest call to commitment that can be found in all of the Gospels. Insofar as our religious mood has shifted from dogma to concern, and from correctness of theological affirmation to the urgency of commitment, these are the words which speak directly to our age. The central call to Christian commitment is phrased in the words, "Take my yoke upon you." The terms are the terms of recruitment.

Once we face, with honesty, the burdened character of human life, we are bound to seek an answer to the problem that is involved. The fact that we live in a rich and comfortable land does not by any means absolve us. Indeed life can be exceedingly painful even to those who are materially fortunate. The inventions of modern civilization, while they may have altered the proportions of misfortune, have certainly not eliminated it and will not eliminate it. Inventions do not change in any thorough way the human situation, because they are neither the cause nor the cure of man's troubles. If insecurity arose merely from external conditions, these conditions might eventually be altered, but this is not how our worst troubles arise. The worst troubles arise from the thoughts and decisions and emotions of men, including ourselves.

It is in the light of such facts that the religious answer to the demand for comfort is made. Thus we have the beginning of a great passage in Isaiah: "Comfort ye, comfort ye my people, saith our God." The broken, the refugees, the desolate, the defeated, and the desperate have a right to know that in the love of God there is ultimate solace and indeed the only such solace which they will ever find.

Only a person of very hard heart will ever minimize this aspect of religious experience. There are the blind; there are the deaf; there are the dumb; there are the lame; and all of them are entitled to know that the hand of God is reaching out tenderly to them. Charles Wesley was working at the main theme of all great faith when he taught men to sing:

13

Hear Him, ye deaf; his praise, ye dumb,
Your loosened tongues employ;
Ye blind, behold your Saviour come;
And leap, ye lame, for joy!

Important and necessary as the theme of comfort is, it can never be the only theme if our religious vitality is to be maintained. There is another theme found strongly in the cumulative message of the prophets of Israel, which seems to be at complete variance with the theme of comfort. By it people are aroused from their complacency, they are disturbed by new ideas, they are driven out of all safe nests and sometimes sent long distances on arduous tasks which they would never willingly choose for themselves.

John the Baptist belonged to this prophetic tradition in that his message was one calculated to arouse rather than to comfort. Instead of overcoming people's fears, he added to their fears and, to the conventionally pious who listened to him, he said, "You brood of vipers." He reminded them that the chaff would be burned with unquenchable fire. If John gave any word of comfort to the bereaved and the perplexed we do not know what it was.

We sometimes forget that in the teaching of Christ Himself there was this strain which seems to be absolutely antithetical to the gospel of comfort. A gospel it undoubtedly is, but it does not sound like good news. The same sort of people who were called a brood of vipers by John were called the same by Christ. He also called them "Whited sepulchers." They were told that they appeared outwardly righteous, while in reality they were full of hypocrisy and iniquity. They claimed to be teachers of others, but Christ called them blind guides. He was not drying their tears, allaying their fears, or giving them courage for the day.

The strongest passage in which Christ proclaims the theme

14

of anti-comfort is that in which he develops the figure of the sword. "Do not think," He says, "that I have come to bring peace on earth; I have not come to bring peace, but a sword." In order to make His meaning utterly clear, and to show that His reference to the sword is purely figurative, He goes on to show how disturbing the gospel can be. It can drive people out of all earthly security; it can arouse; it can shake; it can pull asunder.

This phase of Christ's teaching is today utterly shocking to many people. Indeed it is so shocking that there are Christian circles in which it is never mentioned at all. Some persons, who think of themselves as familiar with the Christian faith, actually express surprise when they hear, as for the first time, Christ's words, "Do not think that I came to bring peace on earth." They wonder if something is wrong or if this is a misquotation. "How can this be made consistent," they ask, "with the familiar picture of the lowly Nazarene, healing the sick, comforting the lonely, speaking tenderly to little children?"

However shocking the theme of the Christian sword may be, a little thought will convince us that it is a valid theme. There are many ways in which the gospel, far from making life easier, makes it harder. This may be seen, for example, in the matter of money. To enter Christ's cause does not ordinarily lead to making more money. Indeed it frequently leads to a life in which the disciple makes less, because he cares about many other things as a consequence of his new devotion and not just about making money. Frequently he comes to value much in life that takes away his power of making money. And even when he gets money, his love of the gospel drives him to give away a great deal of it. He knows that a man's true life does not consist in the things that he possesses. He is no longer as free as he was and he is especially not free to use all of his own resources to satisfy his own selfish interests or for his own comfort. The person who gives money to the church because he thinks that as a consequence more will come back to him, and in the end he will be richer, has not even begun to understand what the gospel means.

In a similar way the gospel may disturb family life. However deeply we may believe in the recovery of the family and in the wonder and joy which it can represent, it is nevertheless true that a real Christian commitment is frequently a divisive element in family life. There are persons who are drawn to discipleship, but who hold back because of what the family might think. Often the family would be ashamed of such apparent fanaticism. A good many young men, who choose the Christian ministry, enter it against the desires of their fathers and mothers, who wish their sons to be successful men in a secular society. Jesus seemed to understand all this perfectly when He warned those who would follow Him against the supposition that the path would be easy, by saying that a man's foes might be those of his own household.

The most striking area in which a vital Christianity fails to give comfort is in peace of mind and this, no doubt, is what Jesus meant when He said: "Do not suppose that I came to bring peace." Certainly He was not talking about peace between nations. The easy way to have peace of mind is to feel virtuous and righteous. Then there is a notable sense of peace. Such an assumption of righteousness is commonly found in pagan circles, whether ancient or modern. The natural man tends to believe that he is doing pretty well, that he is loving and kind, and that he is fulfilling his responsibilities as well as could reasonably be expected.

Even a small dose of vital Christianity is enough to shake people out of their easy complacency. When they begin to measure themselves by the standard of Christ, they know that their own personal goodness is poor and shoddy by comparison. Jesus taught all who would learn to pray, not to be satisfied with their moral self-improvement, but to ask forgiveness for sins. A Christian is one who, among other things, admits daily that he has done those things which he ought not to have done and left undone those things which he ought to have done. Instead of thanking God that he is not as others, he cries out in sincerity, "God be merciful to me, a sinner."

In many areas the gospel, instead of taking away people's burdens, actually adds to them. John Woolman's burdens were multiplied when his deep religious experience brought him to the realization that slavery was evil and contrary to the will of God. After that he could not rest throughout the remainder of his life. In an essentially similar, though less dramatic way, modest lives are every day made more complex by accepting the lordship of Christ. Men are forced to find new forms of ministry and to promote new causes. Occasionally we talk of our Christianity as something that solves problems, and there is a sense in which it does. Long before it does so, however, it increases both the number and the intensity of the problems. Even our intellectual questions are increased by the acceptance of a strong religious faith. The unbeliever is not, for example, bothered by what we call the problem of evil. He is not disturbed by the existence of unmerited suffering in the world, because he has no faith with which this suffering appears to be incompatible. His philosophy may be for more superficial than that of the Christian, but, just because it is usually simpler, it is more easily held without a sense of tragic tension. If a man wishes to avoid the disturbing effect of paradoxes, the best advice is for him to leave the Christian faith alone.

Here then is what appears to be real conflict within the

classic religious heritage, steeped as it is in Biblical faith. On the one hand there is the call for comfort, while, on the other, there is the call for disturbance. How can the two be combined, without contradiction, in a valid system of life and faith? On the surface this looks impossible, since the two moods appear to be wholly incompatible. It is in the solution of this problem that much of the true glory of the gospel appears, for Christ is able to take us to a deeper level in which both of the valid, yet radically opposed, demands are met simultaneously. The method which Christ uses to accomplish this end involves the marvelous figure of the yoke.

The great yoke passage, which is found at the end of the eleventh chapter of Matthew, begins with the recognition of the validity of the demand for comfort. We see how tender Christ was with all the broken and the needy when He began the great pronouncement by saying, "Come unto me all ye who labor and are heavy laden and I will give you rest." This appears to be the theme of comfort, pure and simple, so that we naturally expect Christ to go on and say that the heavy-laden must lay down their burdens, but this is precisely what He does not say. In a really shocking paradox Christ offers rest to the burdened by asking them to share His burden. His solution of the problem of those who are tired with toil is to offer them the world's greatest symbol of toil; namely, the yoke. The yoke means, in some places, that by which a man can, through a device on his shoulders, carry more than he could otherwise carry. In other places it means the harness which animals, either oxen or asses, wear, by which they are able to pull a plow.[2] In any case, the striking fact is that Christ's offer of peace was through the acceptance of new responsibilities and that His offer of rest was through

[2] See *Dictionary of the Bible*, edited by James Hastings, p. 16.

the voluntary sharing of new toil. He did not say that He Himself would remove burdens. What He did say was that, because His yoke was perfectly fitted, His own burden seemed light.

Here we come to the very heart of the paradox of the Christian gospel. The preaching of rest alone is a heresy, and the preaching of disturbance alone is a heresy. There is something better than the Second Isaiah and likewise there is something better than John the Baptist. What we seek is a life in which both rest and disturbance come, and come in a way which is not contradictory, because both arise from the deep commitment to Christ and His Kingdom. It may take all of our lives to find out what this means, and no doubt we shall never know fully, but, in the idea of Christ's yoke, we have our fundamental clue which can lead to the practical solution of our problem. Comfort comes, but it comes neither lightly nor easily nor quickly. It comes at long last and often after much tragedy and pain. Disturbance we must have, but it is never mere disturbance, because we know that underneath there are the everlasting arms. New burdens we must carry, but they can be carried with a triumphant and overcoming joy. We are well on the road toward the fullness of the Christian life when we realize that the paradox of the yoke is the paradox of the gospel.

There may be ways in which references to the simple gospel are accurate, but the paradox of the yoke is not one of them. The answer of the secular psychiatrist, who tries to eliminate a man's sense of guilt instead of seeking to have it both recognized and transcended by reference to the divine forgiveness, is really a far simpler gospel than is the gospel of Christ, and its very simplicity is a mark of its inadequacy. The yoke is a more complex symbol than is the couch. The Christian answer lies, not in the achievement of the easy conscience, but in the achievement of new life.

Because we are accustomed to the phrase "Take my yoke upon you," having heard it often in Handel's *Messiah* if nowhere else, the great words are no longer shocking to us, but they must have been terribly shocking to those who first heard them. Even our acceptance of the words does not mean acceptance of the idea. Perhaps this is why the symbol of the yoke has been so much less common in Christian history than have the other symbols suggested by Christ's own words. The yoke appears, it is true, in a somewhat disguised form in the clergyman's stole, and during the last few years it has begun to be used as a lapel pin, but for the most part it has been neglected. In contrast, the cross and the cup have been used abundantly in nearly all groups of Christians. A yoke appears in one window of the Seminary Chapel at Gettysburg, but such use is rare.

The neglect of the yoke is understandable when we realize the degree to which it is an affront to our ordinary wishes. Christ does not give us the answer which we naturally desire to have. We want to escape responsibility, but Christ will not let us do so. In both the yoke and the cross He took ideas which must have been revolting to many of His hearers, and transformed them by adding new meaning. In using the word, Christ undoubtedly had something of the rabbinical tradition in mind, according to which a student symbolically accepted the teacher's yoke; however, the major Old Testament connotation of yoke was evil, referring to bondage. In any case, Christ picked up the figure and gave it a new and liberating significance.

The heart of the transvaluation comes in the note of joy. Real freedom, Christ says, is not the absence of limitations on our actions, but the joyous acceptance of limitations inherent in the new loyalty. As a result there comes a liberation

20

greater than any merely empty or irresponsible freedom can ever bring. The yoke, instead of being a galling instrument, is consequently a harness which is easy to wear. We do not seek peace directly, but it comes ultimately as a by-product of the act of giving ourselves unreservedly to Christ's cause.

We are made to be spent. This is inherent in the very nature of the human situation. The revolting symbol of the yoke, feared and rejected by many Christians even to this day, comes to stand for the chief meaning of the Christian life. What is a Christian? A Christian is one who seeks, in spite of his failures, to wear Christ's yoke with Him. This is not the conclusion of the gospel, but it is a big step on the way. It takes a great deal of thinking to understand in detail what the wearing of the yoke must mean, but at least we know where to start. There is something better than comfort, and there is something better than disturbance. As we try to wear Christ's yoke with Him, we begin to learn what it is.

THE SALT OF THE EARTH

You are the salt of the earth; but if salt has lost its taste, how can its saltness be restored? It is no longer good for anything except to be thrown out and trodden under foot by men.
MATTHEW 5:13

The greatest sermon in all the world was given to one of the smallest companies. Sometimes we see reproductions of the supposed scene of the Sermon on the Mount with vast numbers of people on the mountain, but this is not what the Biblical account suggests. "Seeing the crowds, Jesus went up into a mountain, and when he had sat down, his disciples came to him and he opened his mouth and taught them." We have no way of knowing that all of the material now grouped together in the fifth, sixth, and seventh chapters of Matthew's gospel was ever combined in one single address, but the beginning was clearly preached to a small group. It is reasonable to suppose that Christ said similar things, with variations, on different occasions and certainly there were other references to salt (Mark 9:49, 50 and Luke 14:34, 35), but the reference in the Sermon on the Mount is unique in its identification of the Christian community with the saving salt.

The statement of Christ which follows immediately after the Beatitudes is really amazing. What Jesus says is that there is a special way in which the world can be kept from decay and that the world is to be saved by a particular kind of penetration. In the days of Christ the only way to preserve meat was by the use of salt. By this practice, then as now, meat could be kept a long time. Christ began with the recognition that human civilization is always in danger of decay. It can go to pieces very easily; in fact, the natural movement of the world is often a movement of decline. Soil tends to erode unless conscious effort is made to retain it and standards of human conduct go down unless laborious efforts are made to maintain them. When society drifts of itself, it always drifts in the same direction. It is easy to lose any kind of excellence, whether academic, religious, scientific, or political. Civilization continues only when it is the object of vigilant solicitude. Therefore we must, if we care, find a way to preserve what is valuable and to maintain what is worthy. What was amazing was Christ's calm assertion that the tiny group of disciples on the mountainside were the ones who could preserve the world. Superficially this was absurd. If you had been a Roman citizen, with some knowledge of history and of the Empire, and somebody had told you that this tiny group of men, with perhaps some women, on this Palestinian mountain, already had within them the means of redeeming contemporary civilization and influencing the future civilization of the world, you would have found the idea laughable. It would have been laughable because it appeared that these people had absolutely nothing on their side. Of course they had a young inspiring leader, but you would certainly have predicted that, with His death, the bubble would burst. Like Gamaliel you might reasonably have referred to Theudas or Judas the Galilean or others like them:

For before these days Theudas arose, giving himself out to be somebody, and a number of men, about four hundred, joined him;

but he was slain and all who followed him were dispersed and came to nothing. After him Judas the Galilean arose in the days of the census and drew away some of the people after him; he also perished, and all who followed him were scattered. [Acts 5:36, 37].

Christ's disciples were in a remote part of the Roman Empire, having no standing, no money, no prestige, no worldly power, no education. Consequently, from a human point of view, the chance of their enduring was very slight, while the idea that they could redeem or save the civilization of the world was obviously fantastic.

In spite of all such considerations, Jesus made His tremendous prediction. His statement was paradoxical, but what is far more paradoxical is the fact. Nearly all of the rest of the things on which men depended did actually decay. The Roman Empire did come to an end; Plato's Academy finally closed; the great library at Alexandria was finally burned; the legions were scattered; the schools of the Stoics and the Epicureans faded out. But the little redemptive society which Christ instituted as the divine preservative went on. It entrenched itself in the Greco-Roman world; it penetrated Caesar's household; it carried men through the Dark Ages; it survived the Renaissance, the Reformation, the Enlightenment, and the Industrial Revolution, as it is now surviving the Atomic Revolution. Your presence here thousands of miles from the place where the original pronouncement was made, is one modest evidence that it is still going on. The incredible has occurred.

The fact of enduring preservation is one which we can never overestimate. Apparently Jesus had a perfectly clear understanding of the means of redemption, and perhaps this is what He was thinking out when He was alone in the desert. He knew that His body would be destroyed, and although

24

He knew that He would arise again, He also knew that the time would come when His earthly existence, in the form in which it had continued for thirty years, would be no more. How then would the work go on? He must have toyed with the idea of writing a book. That is what so many have done, but He did not write. We know of no case of His writing except when He wrote in the sand with His finger, near the woman who was taken in adultery, but we do not know what He wrote. He did not leave a book; He did not leave an army; He did not leave an organization, in the ordinary sense. What He left, instead, was a little redemptive fellowship made up of extremely common people whose total impact was miraculous. Though the members were individually unworthy, the fellowship which they came to share was so far superior to the sum of its parts that it was not only able to survive and endure, but finally to dominate and to save. We are beginning to understand why Christ spent most of His time, in His mature ministry, with the *twelve*. A great many of the parables were told, not to the crowds who, after all, faded away, but to this little handful of men, as though to say, "The only hope is so to fill them that the group will go on." The miracle is that it did go on, and this is how the gospel made its impact upon the ancient world.

It is hard for us to visualize what early Christianity was like. Certainly it was very different from the Christianity known to us today. There were no fine buildings. In most places there were, in fact, no Christian buildings at all. There was no hierarchy; there were no theological seminaries; there were no Christian colleges; there were no Sunday Schools; there were no choirs. Only small groups of believers—small fellowships. In the beginning there wasn't even a New Testament. The New Testament itself was not so much a cause of these fellowships as a result of them. Thus the first books of the New Testament were the letters written to the little fellowships partly because of their difficulties, dangers, and temptations. All that they had was the fellowship; nothing else; no standing; no prestige; no honor. For a long time practically none were citizens of the Roman Empire. The citizenship of Paul was stressed partly because it was so rare. It was actually true, and not mere rhetoric, to say, "Not many of you were wise according to worldly standards, not many were powerful, not many were of noble birth" (I Cor. 1:26). The early Christians were not people of standing, but they had a secret power among them, and the secret power resulted from the way in which they were members one of another.

Can you think now of what it must have been like? One little fellowship was meeting in a house in Philippi, another was gathered in a house or a rented place or a synagogue in Corinth. In Ephesus the fellowship met in a rented place, a school building, but mostly Christians gathered in homes. That is why one of the most precious terms in the New Testament is "the church that is in their house." At first the rest of this world hardly knew that they existed, for they made no great stir. It was only at Thessalonica that the early Christians were accused of turning the world upside down. For the most part they did not seem subversive, though they really were. In the helpful words of a modern expositor,

There is no despair because the group is small: a pinch of salt is effective out of all proportion to its amount. There is no hermit strategy: the disciples are to stay in the world, touching even its unworthy life, if they would redeem it. There is no call to a sensational witness: salt is inconspicuous, ordinary and admixed with common things.[1]

[1] *The Interpreters' Bible*, Vol. VII, p. 289.

The little redemptive societies did their work just as Christ had taught in the parables of the mustard seed and the leaven which appear together in the gospel:

The kingdom of heaven is like to a grain of mustard seed, which a man took, and sowed in his field: which indeed is the least of all seeds: but when it is grown, it is the greatest among herbs, and becometh a tree, so that the birds of the air come and lodge in the branches thereof.

Another parable spake he unto them: The kingdom of heaven is like unto leaven, which a woman took, and hid in three measures of meal, till the whole was leavened [AV].

Sometimes, in a preaching mission, we are discouraged because nearly all of those who attend are already dedicated, at least in some measure, to the promotion of Christ's Kingdom. We wish we could have the others present. But the deepening of the already dedicated is, in the light of Christ's method, a matter of great importance. It is through the dedicated ones, as they become more loving and more infectious, that the world is to be changed. The world is what we seek to influence, but the truth of the gospel is that it is the concentrated "little" which affects the diffused "big." The gospel conquers the world by the establishment of small strong points. The Kingdom makes no direct onslaught, but occupies points and moves out from them into surrounding territory.

What occurred in the ancient civilization was the organic development of the fellowship, but never a merely individual Christianity. That would not have been able to survive. The fellowship was the only thing that could win. The early Christians came together to strengthen one another and to encourage one another in their humble gatherings such as are described in I Corinthians, Chapter 14, and then they went out into their ministry in the Greco-Roman world, until they were finally able to touch every part of it educationally, politically, culturally, and morally. All of these parts were touched because the fellowship itself had such intensity, such vitality, and such power. This was the method; this was the victory; and this is why we are here as Christians nineteen hundred years and more later.

What is the contemporary relevance of the original Christian story? It appears in the recognition that the paganism of our time is not likely to be countered and met in any other way than in the way by which the paganism of the Greco-Roman world was countered and met. Christ's method is still our method; it is still our hope. The task before Christians is the re-enactment of the fundamental miracle.

Jesus recognized that although the only way to preserve the world was by this particular kind of salt, there was also a way in which it could be lost. At first it is difficult for us to understand Christ's reference to the loss of saltness, because we know from our chemical studies that pure salt is always salt. It does not lose its saltness. Pure sodium chloride does not deteriorate. What then did He mean? The salt with which Christ was familiar was a crude composite such as would be familiar on the shores of the Dead Sea or the Mediterranean Sea. This salt could be so adulterated as to be essentially lost. A great deal of it would not be salt at all, but other crude material, and it would stand in piles, not so different from those which we can see today on the shores of San Francisco Bay, where the salt is heaped up before it is refined. As these piles would stand out in the open in the rain, frequently the salt would be washed out and nothing would remain but the dross, with no true saltness left. The point of Christ's words is that the residue is absolutely worthless. It is not worth a little; it is worth nothing! It is only to be trodden, He said, under the feet of men. And this is clearly what He means concerning the redemptive society which we call the church. If all of the salt is washed out of it, if all that is left is just the worldly emphasis of respectability and fine buildings, an ecclesiastical structure and conventional religion with the redemptive power gone, it isn't partly good; it isn't any good.

Christ is saying that mild religion, far from being of partial value, is of utterly no value. We can lose our Christianity! It is easy to go on with the motions; it is easy to continue a structure; it is easy to go on with a system. But Christ says it isn't worth a thing. Eroded religion is of no value at all. The consequence for us is that the Christian religion must mean far more, or it will eventually mean nothing.

The brief passage about the salt is as remarkable for its realism as it is for its exciting hope. Within the same context we find both the plan of redemption and the clear recognition of possible failure in spite of apparent success. A religion which has lost its sense of concern and becomes a mere means of personal comfort is one which Christ is bound to renounce, even if it uses His name and claims to maintain historical continuity with the beginnings of Christianity. He would throw it out and give it no attention at all. Herein lies what may be called the toughness of Christ. He refuses to waste time and effort on worn-out causes.

That Christ was completely realistic about the possibility and the seriousness of failure of any society, including a Christian society, is shown by His use of another parable—that of the barren fig tree—to make the same point as that of the worthlessness of the pile from which the true salt had been drained away. There is no virtue, He taught, in continuing to be patient with what is hopelessly unproductive.

A man had a fig tree planted in his vineyard; and he came seeking fruit on it and found none. And he said to the vinedresser,

"Lo, these three years I have come seeking fruit on this fig tree, and I find none. Cut it down; why should it use up the ground?" [Luke 13:6, 7]

In the light of this combined teaching, a Christian must always be both tough and tender. He must be tender with new life as it grows up in hope, but he must, at the same time, be aware of the waste of trying to keep alive what is intrinsically a dying movement. If Christian movements grow up for awhile and later seem to have come upon periods of decay, that is not wholly surprising. Probably it is a better use of our time to start something new than it is to try to nourish that from which the major power is gone. It is better, in many cases, to plant a new tree than to bother endlessly with one which is really hopeless.

We are glad that Christ is thus wonderfully realistic about His sacred fellowship, but what is thrilling is that its power is never wholly lost. When it seems to be lost at one point in the Christian fellowship, it springs up in another, and often in an unexpected sector. The salt never wholly loses its saltness. There is, in the world, a great deal of decay, but the preservative is itself miraculously preserved.

We can be sobered and humbled by the recognition that even at this late date, Christ can use people like ourselves in performing His redemptive work of keeping the world from full decay. Christ's word to the little group on the mountainside is also His word to every little church, every little Christian society, every fellowship in His cause. To us as to them comes the assurance that in His service we can be more than we are. The claim is still incredible, and it is still true.

THE GATES OF HELL

Upon this rock I will build my church, and the gates of hell shall not prevail against it.   MATTHEW 16:18, AV

No one who is seeking to become a disciple of Jesus Christ can afford to neglect the passage in the sixteenth chapter of Matthew's gospel in which the first mention of the church is recorded. The passage is important to Roman Catholics, but it is also important to Protestants and to all others who are serious about sharing actively in the Christian undertaking. Though there is not full agreement about the significance of the key words, there is general agreement that the passage is crucial. The experience of Christ and the intimate group in the region of Caesarea-Philippi seems to have been a true watershed in Christ's public ministry and in the thought of the disciples. After that all was different and, though the understanding of the Twelve was still dim, they undoubtedly saw subsequent events in a new light.

So far as we know, the passage in question includes Christ's first reference to His church. The idea must have been baffling because of its very novelty. We have heard of the church ever since, but, at that time, no one had heard of it at all. There are points of newness in human history, points at which novelty emerges, and this was one of them.

It is thoroughly surprising to most contemporary Christians

31

to learn how nearly unique the church is. We tend to assume that because we have it, all people have it or at least have something roughly similar to it. We speak normally of the Christian Church, but the phrase is highly redundant because, if we are strict in our usage, there is no other. A brilliant and charming Buddhist monk came recently to the United States from Cambodia and gave generously of his time to explain the religious and cultural life of his people, lecturing especially on the Buddhist faith. In one group of educated people, those who listened to him were grateful for what he said, but were surprised at the end that he had not said anything about his church. All realized that they, if they were in a foreign culture and lecturing on Christianity, would have mentioned their local church in the beginning. It seemed to them a perfectly natural starting place. They wondered why the Buddhist did not do the same. Soon it dawned upon them that the reason was very simple. He did not tell about his church because there was none.

The Buddhist monk told, in an interesting way, of the life of the monks and of the life of the nuns. He explained both their sense of vocation and the rigorous discipline by which their lives are guided. He told interestingly of the Buddhist Scriptures, of the emphasis on human love, and of the shrines. But none of these represents the church as it is known in Christian experience, for the church is not monks and nuns and Scriptures and shrines. The church is the gathered community, the household of faith, the regular coming together of ordinary men and women who are fathers and mothers and holders of jobs. It is because of the peculiar idea of the church as a redemptive fellowship that the characteristic physical structure of Christianity is not a temple or a wayside shrine, but a *meetinghouse*.

The more we study, the more we realize that Christ's

emphasis upon the saving fellowship is really unique among the religions of the world. The emphasis upon the gathered community as the major religious unit is not matched in other faiths and is only partially seen, in advance of the Christian Era, in the prophetic development of the synagogue of the Jewish dispersion. Before Christ's coming the characteristic religious experience of most of those of the pagan world was that of solitariness before the shrine rather than that of two or three together. When the Apostle Paul noted, in Athens, that the people were very religious, he was not referring to any evidence of an experience similar to that of a church gathered week by week, but rather to the altars to which men and women made pious visits one by one.

There is some tendency in the modern world to encourage the kind of religion in which each goes alone to pray before a candle or a statue or an altar, the chief encouragement being provided by the building of little chapels, conveniently located, into which people can walk directly from busy streets. A great many of the new places have included small chapels especially designed for a religious exercise which is essentially individual, even though several persons may be doing it at the same time. No one who cares seriously about the spiritual life of our time can oppose such a development; but insofar as he has any real inkling of what Christ was trying to accomplish, he must insist loudly that such individual worship is insufficient and far removed from what is most valuable in Christian experience. Bowing before a shrine is really a throwback to the pre-Christian conception of the nature of religion.

In is impossible to overstress the value of the meetinghouse in the development of Christian civilization. Neither the Jewish Temple at Jerusalem nor the Parthenon in Athens was a meetinghouse in the sense of a building made specifically for the use of the beloved community. Each was a place of prayer, but the prayer envisaged was not that of the gathered fellowship. The emphasis was not upon the people, but upon the physical setting. The power in the steady coming together, week by week, of the living fellowship was neither understood nor expected prior to the time when the destruction of the Temple forced the formation of the synagogue. Even then the conception was not fully developed; the synagogue was the beginning, but only the beginning, of the idea of the church.

The emphasis on the church is one of the chief ways in which Christ made it clear that He was trying to do something radically different from anything done by the Hebrew prophets or by their fiery successor, John the Baptist. Outside observers naturally thought of Him in this tradition, but finally discovered their mistake. The Baptist undoubtedly had some good ideas and he expressed them well, but there is no evidence that he built a society. Though he did have a few followers who, the New Testament tells us, endured for a while, we have no reason to believe that John encouraged a conscious fellowship comparable to that of the Twelve. Indeed, we should never have heard of the words of the Baptist if the conscious fellowship started by Christ had not preserved, along with the words of Christ, some of those of His immediate predecessor. Crucial to our understanding of the gospel is Christ's reference to the Baptist after John had been committed to prison. What Jesus said about His remarkable predecessor leads up to the memorable section in which Christ makes His clearest call to commitment, inviting all who are weary and heavy laden, not merely to repent, but to become partners in the redemptive fellowship by wearing His yoke with Him. The key to the whole discourse is Matthew 11:11, in which Christ, in spite of all His admiration for John, points out the radical difference between what John was trying to do and what the essential Christian strategy is. "Truly, I say to you, among those born of women there has risen no one greater than John the Baptist; yet he who is least in the kingdom of heaven is greater than he." The difference was the difference between a noble voice and a redemptive society.

Once the central idea of changing the world by means of a divinely perpetuated society was clear, the practical problem was that of the makeup of this society. Should it be of men only, of monks only, of scholars only? Would it be a Christian version of Plato's Academy? The answer, as everyone knows, led in a radically different direction. It is one thing to have an architect's plan of a building, but it is quite another to decide upon the materials and to do the actual work of construction. On what kind of stuff, Christ seems to have asked, would He or could He build His church? The shocking answer was that He would build on the poor human stuff that He saw right in front of Him.

The long discussion between Protestants and Roman Catholics about the meaning of the Rock has been almost as unprofitable as it has been acrimonious. It is conceivable that the conventional answer of both groups has been wrong. The standard Roman Catholic answer is that the reference to the rock was Christ's way of establishing the institution of the papacy. The simple argument is that Christ was intending to set up an ecclesiastical hierarchy, that He determined to begin this with Simon Peter, as the leader of the Apostles, and that there has been an unbroken succession reaching from Simon to the present Pope. Though we may grant that this argument is impressive to the ignorant, it is really difficult to see how a thoughtful person can teach it with any sincerity, because the logic is faulty. Some of the weak points are the following: First, Christ was clearly opposed to the whole idea of a hierarchy, fought the established religious leadership of His time, and made the point abundantly clear by the flat rejection of such titles as "Father" and "Rabbi." Second, Peter was not only a married man, since Christ healed his mother-in-law and Paul referred to Peter's habit of taking his wife with him, but he was also an extremely poor example of moral strength, let alone theological inerrancy. Furthermore, there is no specific mention of the papacy or any succession on any page of the New Testament. The leap from Peter as the acknowledged leader of a little band of Apostles to the recognition of a great religious and secular leader to whom all other Christians must be subservient is a logical leap of such magnitude that it is really hard to see how honest people can make it.

On the other hand, the standard Protestant answer avoids the basic question. The ordinary solution consists in saying that the Rock was not Peter the man, but Peter's confession of the divine Lordship of Christ. The trouble with this answer is that it was the man and not the doctrine that was given the name of rock. Not only was the nickname given to an individual, but also it was made to stick. Often, as the other Apostles used the name in subsequent years, they must have been reminded of the important discussion when the first mention of Christ's church was made.

If we agree that it is more honest to see the term rock applied to a person than to an idea, what can the meaning be? Undoubtedly the first reaction of the Apostles was laughter. It is a shame that we are so impressed with the terrible seriousness of the gospel that we fail to laugh when laughter is in order. To call Simon "Rocky" was humorous because he was among the most unstable of men. His instability was vividly demonstrated by his denial of Christ when the going was hard immediately prior to the crucifixion. Undoubtedly then, to call Simon the rock when he was really rubble was roughly similar to our ordinary practice of calling the fat man Slim and the tall man Shorty. All would understand and appreciate the joke. Yet the joke was more than a joke. It was on the poor rubble of ordinary human nature that Christ would actually depend. He did not wait for the emergence of the elite: he started with what was everywhere available. And the enduring truth is that it is still such stuff as Peter represented that Christ uses to build His church. He began, not with a society of monks, but with common men and women who constituted the household of faith. What is really amazing is the way in which a structure, built of such inadequate materials, has continued through all vicissitudes. It has survived in spite of persecution and inner corruption and self-seeking and humiliating division.

Even more surprising than Christ's announcement of the stuff on which He would build is His bold prediction of the outcome. But here is the point at which we need to be particularly careful if we are not to misunderstand Him completely. It is undoubtedly true that most Christians, when they think of the phrase about the gates of hell not being able to prevail, picture the church as on the defensive. They see the church as a great castle, standing on a rock, with a moat about it, and with enemies attacking from every side. The enemies, who are the agents of the hellish assault, are wily and persistent, but their efforts are always unavailing. The church continues to stand through all attacks, because the rock is firm, the moat is not crossed, and the vigilance is never relaxed.

However appealing this defensive picture is, and however common it is in our imagination, it is not the picture indicated by the text we are considering. The more we study Christ's words, the more we are sure that He was thinking of His church as eternally on the offensive. It is the gates of hell, not the gates of the church, that are being stormed, and the good news is that the gates of hell cannot always be impervious to the Christian attack. The redemptive fellowship, Christ seems to say, is on the offensive, and it is so strong in its penetration that even the very gates of hell cannot keep it from entering. Perhaps this is one reason why the expression, "He descended into Hell," found its way into the Apostles' Creed. The glorious faith is that no gate, not even a gate of Hell, can remain permanently shut if the redemptive group, centered in Christ, is sufficiently faithful. The gates of hell are many, but we know some of them very well. They are the gates of prejudice and hatred and ignorance and self-centeredness. All of these must be stormed and all of these can be stormed. They cannot hold out forever.

The confusion in Christian circles, which the conventional defensive conception has caused, is both pathetic and amusing. For example, the current edition of the *Presbyterian Hymnal* presents two antithetical pictures on two facing pages, numbered 164 and 165. On the left of these two pages is the hymn beginning, "The strife is o'er," which includes the line:

He closed the yawning gates of hell,

but, on the right, we find Charles Wesley's "Christ the Lord is Risen Today," with a more robust conception expressed in the line:

Christ hath burst the gates of hell.

Our hope is that Wesley's interpretation will become the dominant one, because it seems to be more faithful to the original gospel.

The grand passage about the gates of hell really turns out to be a passage devoted to Christian strategy. What is needed always is a firm center from which we can start and to which we may need to return for reinvigoration, but most of the time must be spent in less congenial places. The chief ministry of concerned Christians must be carried on, not in churches and not in the midst of the delightful fellowship of the like-minded, but in the market places and in various parts of secular society. The classic pattern is that of Columba, who established his permanent base on the beautiful island of Iona in the Inner Hebrides, but who expected his fellow workers to spend most of their time on the Scottish mainland, engaged in the arduous task of the Conversion of Scotland. Men need both a base and a field. It is wrong to remain always at the base and it is wrong to remain always in the field. The strategy is to repair to the base of the sacred fellowship from time to time for spiritual renewal, but then to return at once to the difficult task of penetrating the secular order. The service begins when the meeting ends.

The Apostolate of any day must be made up of people who are seeking to carry the spirit of Christ into common life, particularly in their daily work. Often in the past, by our undue emphasis upon what was called full-time Christian service, we have distorted the fundamental Christian strategy. All the gates need to be stormed. All kinds of organizations are ready for penetration. Thus we need a great many deeply committed librarians because, thereby, the standard of reading may be lifted. It goes without saying that such people must have technical competence as well as Christian enthusiasm. The same goes for politics and any other job.

Perhaps the idea of commitment in common life indicates

the chief way in which our educational problem will finally be solved. It is increasingly difficult to find able teachers to go into the separate schools established for the lazy and the cruel. The offering of money is not likely to succeed, particularly in drawing out the kind of educational talent that is required. In the long run the only solution lies in the quality of commitment. The time may come when brave and dedicated young men and women will undertake the hardest jobs in teaching, in the same mood that others have demonstrated in the past in volunteering to serve in colonies for lepers. The motive of commitment may accomplish what the financial motive can never accomplish.

On another level we need many Christian scholars who, whatever their fields of competence, will enter the work of university teaching, realizing that, in many departments, they will be outnumbered by colleagues who look upon the Christian faith as an outworn superstition. Often the teacher can be more effective if he enters the university service as a professor of psychology, where the going is hard, than if he enters the field of Biblical studies, where the going is comparatively easy. This is because the task of the church is the penetration of all of life.

The upshot of the crucial passage of the sixteenth chapter of Matthew is, then, the recognition of the true nature of the church. Christians exist, not primarily to comfort and to buttress one another, but to penetrate the world. Christianity, whenever it is true to itself, is a movement with a powerful thrust. The church is many things, but primarily it is a Society of Jesus, made up of ordinary people penetrating ordinary life.

THE
KEYS
OF THE
KINGDOM

I will give you the keys of the king-dom of heaven, and whatever you bind on earth shall be bound in heaven, and whatever you loose on earth shall be loosed in heaven.
Matthew 16:19

Christ's reference to the keys of the kingdom is almost as well known and almost as controversial as is His reference to the rock on which His church is built. The references to keys and rock appear only once in the New Testament, and they appear in the same story. Both are enigmatic, yet both, if carefully studied, may shed great light upon the inner nature of the gospel. The best discoveries may come where the digging is hardest.

One possible meaning of the keys is familiar to millions in the Christian world. This may be stated simply, yet not unfairly, as follows: Christ was concerned with preparing a system by which people would gain access to heaven. With this as the chief interest, it was necessary to set up some arrangement by which it could be determined who would be allowed to enter into heavenly bliss and who would not. The simplest way would be to appoint a keeper of the gate and Jesus decided to appoint the Galilean fisherman, Simon Peter, giving him absolute authority over the eternal destinies of other men. His decisions would, according to

41

this explanation of the passage, be so momentous that what he would decide on earth would be equally decisive in heaven. In short, this man, nicknamed Peter, would have absolute power to forgive sins and thereby to determine the eternal destinies, not only of all his contemporaries, but of the millions yet to be born. Christ was speaking to him, not as a man, but as His earthly vicar. Thus not only the Galilean fisherman, but all of the succeeding bishops of Rome have had in their possession the keys of the kingdom of heaven, with absolute power to allow or to deny entrance. For this reason the Roman Church claims to be the sole possessor of the greatest privilege of the world and is, accordingly, the only church. All others, even when they are centered in Christ and seem to demonstrate the spirit of Christ, showing the fruits of the spirit, are outside the true fold. This is the fundamental reason why Roman Catholics are normally forbidden to share in worship with other Christians. To share would be to recognize. It might give the idea that the monopoly is not absolute.

That this explanation is not a caricature is indicated by the way in which, to this day, Peter is depicted in popular humor as the keeper of the gate of eternal life. We are wise if we study humor to see what the common convictions of men are. Humor is effective only when there are assumptions that do not require explanation. In endless and boring jokes the changeless pattern involves someone dying and appearing at the gate of heaven, with Peter making the decision about entrance through the pearly gates. However lightly we treat this situation, and however grotesque we make it, the endless repetition of the joke at least shows what the popular exegesis of the famous passage is. We may not take seriously the notion of a dictator of eternal destiny for other men, but we tend to think that this is what

Christ's words indicate. We may doubt the truth of what He said, but we do not doubt that the conventional interpretation of the meaning of His words is the correct one.

The place for contemporary Christians to begin is with the meaning. And the reason we must begin there is that the popular or literalistic interpretation of the words is almost certainly incorrect. The chief reason for believing that it is incorrect is that it is radically incompatible with the major tendency of Christ's teaching or with the general teaching of the New Testament. We can be sure, at least, that Christ does not contradict Himself.

We may start by pointing out that the popular interpretation of the famous passage cannot be correct because it is inconsistent with Christ's emphasis on the divine sovereignty. He and the Father are one, He said, but He did not say that Peter and the Father are one. In fact the New Testament is very clear about Peter's personal inadequacy. If Peter, or Peter and his successors, have the absolute power concerning eternal life, how can we account for Christ's assurance to the thief on the cross, "This day wilt thou be with me in Paradise." If the superficial explanation of the passage about the keys had been correct, Christ would have had to ask Peter's permission, but He did not. In fact, Peter was not present, for he was a coward and a defector.

The main current of the gospel teaching is that according to which the Father is seeking to save to the uttermost. The glorious passage in the Book of Revelation, which pictures Christ's eternal knocking at each door, is consistent with the main tenor of His message. It is absurd for Him to go on knocking if it has already been decided, by some human hierarchy, that the door is to be eternally locked. Indeed it is sacrilegious to picture Christ as bestowing patronage powers after the fashion of an earthly ruler. The notion of setting up

43

a system with priestly prerogatives is inconsistent with Christ's well-known opposition to priestly religion in general. In short, we may not know what the reference to the keys really means, but we can at least know that the conventional or superficial explanation is the wrong one.

When we find ourselves in a situation like this, it is a good procedure to back up and to try to see if there are any unstated assumptions which are causing the difficulty. Frequently it is sufficient merely to recognize the assumptions, because they cease to be effective the moment they are clearly presented. For example, the notion of the gospel as merely a heaven-achieving device is one which loses its cogency when it is brought out into the open. Christ, we know, came to help men to live abundantly, and abundant life is needed here and now, quite as much as hereafter. The notion that Christ was setting up a system to determine who would get into heaven and who would not is simply a notion of our manufacture. A second unfounded assumption is that the possession of the keys involves the power to forgive sins or to refuse the forgiveness of sins. Though the two ideas are closely associated in many minds, they are not associated in the gospel record. The connection in Matthew 16 is not between the keys and forgiveness, but between the keys and binding or loosing. The passage about forgiveness appears only in John 20:23 and appears there in such a context that it constitutes a different problem requiring a separate treatment.

An important step has been made, once we rid our minds of the false assumption that the keys refer to forgiveness, but we still need to know what is meant by binding and loosing. Here we are greatly aided by the fact that the phrase about binding and loosing appears a second time in Matthew, in Chapter 18. It is conceivable that Jesus used the theme

more than once, and that Matthew, consequently, gave the
same words in two different settings. So important to our
understanding is the second setting that it is helpful to have
the entire passage before us.

Truly, I say to you, whatever you bind on earth shall be bound
in heaven, and whatever you loose on earth shall be loosed in
heaven. Again I say to you, if two of you agree on earth about anything they ask, it will be done for them by my Father in heaven.
For where two or three are gathered in my name, there am I in
the midst of them. [Matt. 18:18-20]

Here the words about binding and loosing are not addressed to a single man, Peter, but to the Christian group.
This makes it reasonable to suppose that if, in the earlier
setting, Christ was addressing Simon, he was addressing him
not merely as one man, but as a symbol of the kind of persons
on whom, throughout the generations, it would be necessary
for Christ to depend. Peter was symbolic of the poor stuff
out of which the church is built, stuff which, in combination,
is stronger than it is singly and also stronger than it appears
to be. In any case the second use of the words, in another
chapter, is of great assistance to us, because it undermines
any dogmatic claim about the power of one particular man.
The passage may be enigmatic, but it would be far more so
if the reference in Matthew 16 were the only reference.

The most significant feature of the passage in Matthew 18
is the way in which the acts of binding and loosing are re-
lated to the divine fellowship which was being formed by
Christ. The verses which follow immediately are all about
the power and wonder of togetherness. The efficacy of prayer
that is calmly asserted is not that of the prayer of the individual in his aloneness, but of Christians in their togetherness.
This would seem to be the real significance of "two." Two

means "more than one." Following immediately is the well-known promise of the "presence in the midst." The tremendous assertion is that whenever two or three, i.e., the small redemptive fellowship, are gathered in Christ's name, He is actually there with them. Here are no words about a sacred building, no words about an altar with a reserved sacrament, no reference to any ceremonial act. It is neither the place nor the setting nor the ritual that is miraculous; it is the fellowship.

A second great help is available if we connect the words about binding and loosing with Christ's other references to the liberation theme. We know a great deal about Christ's intentions because of what He said and did immediately after His period in the desert when He was meeting temptation and deciding on the major line of His public work. What is so highly significant is His choice of Scripture when He read in the synagogue in His home town. Out of all possible readings, He choose the beginning of Isaiah 61, which is a flaming expression of the liberation theme. As though to give a key to an understanding of His entire message, Jesus read to His neighbors:

He has sent me to proclaim release to the captives and recovering of sight to the blind, to set at liberty those who are oppressed. [Luke 4:18]

Everywhere He saw men who were bound and His purpose was to let them loose.

If we combine these two themes of the fellowship and the liberation we reach a really significant idea. The two themes go perfectly together in the gospel because the fellowship is the loosing agency. Christ came to institute a particular kind of fellowship, the liberating fellowship. Over and over Christ employed brilliant figures to explain this great conception. The figures used in patient explanation were different, but each figure referred to the same reality. The fellowship is the salt which, as it penetrates, keeps from decay; it is the leaven which, as it penetrates, makes the bread to rise; it is the mustard seed which, though it starts small, eventually has a great influence; it is the keys which, though handled by finite men, can open eternal doors.

With the concept of penetration as our clue, we begin to see that there is a way of interpreting the famous words about the keys so that the interpretation is consistent with the bulk of Christ's teaching. The redemptive group, then, is not only the salt which preserves and the leaven which penetrates; it is also the keys which unlock. New possibilities are revealed in human life as the redemptive fellowship grows. The subjection of women cannot continue because the dedicated group will inevitably find a way to take them out of their cultural imprisonment. Men cannot continue forever to hold other men as slaves if the redemptive fellowship becomes a real part of their lives. The very gates of hell, says Christ, cannot remain locked. They can be opened because the redemptive fellowship carries the keys which fit even these locks. Thus the entire passage in Matthew 16 makes sense. The verses are enigmatic when examined alone, but they are not when they are seen together.

This interpretation of the meaning of the famous passage about the keys of the kingdom is in some ways really frightening. It means that those who form and constitute the redemptive fellowship have upon them a very serious responsibility. Christ provided no other means of opening doors in most hearts. He left no other alternative than that involved in the action of the little group to which He gave such affectionate attention and which has been perpetuated through the years, even to our own time. Neither in earth nor in heaven, neither in the present nor in the long future, He suggests, is there any other way. If you do not loose some bonds, perhaps they will not be loosed here or hereafter; if you do not use your God-given key to unlock some door, perhaps it will remain locked, even to all eternity.

In this fashion the words are still shocking, but they cease to seem unchristian. Your responsibility, which extends to all eternity, does not come because somebody appointed you. Peter was not given any special privilege and neither is it given to you or to me. What we face is merely the simple truth that God made the world for fellowship and that fellowship can fail. When it fails the consequences are terrible, and particularly terrible for the innocent. Such failure may not seem fair, but it is involved in the way in which the world is made. I am my brother's keeper. He may be lost if I am unfaithful. Some child may grow up forever ignorant if I refuse to teach.

The responsibility entailed in possessing the keys which may open some other person's life comes to us vividly when we think of what occurred in the life of John R. Mott. This great man influenced the modern world in incalculable ways. It was wholly just that although he was never a politician, he should receive the Nobel Prize for Peace, for he helped to produce the kind of life which goes beyond the mere cessation of fighting. When we think of what he did for the Young's Men's Christian Association, for work among Christian students, for the Church Peace Union, and for the World Council of Churches, we are amazed. But what is more amazing is the fact that all of the Christian ministry of this remarkable layman depended upon his being aroused, and the one who aroused him was a visiting English cricket player whom young Mott met at Cornell. The door which this modest man helped to open was a far larger door than he could possibly have realized. Always the door is larger than the key, but the key is dramatically important. It is important because it is necessary. In Mott's case, the younger man inherited the power of opening, in that his life and words were the means of liberating many who otherwise would not have been freed. Thousands, now living, who heard him at the height of his powers, can bear eloquent witness to the truth of this statement.

What occurred in the relationship between the cricket player and the Cornell student has occurred, in less spectacular ways, in countless situations. This is how the life of the Kingdom grows. In the characteristic situation the person who turns the lock is not even aware that he has done so, but the released man usually knows. It is a common experience to be greatly moved by a sermon and to learn, years afterward, that the person who gave it has utterly forgotten what he said or even that he said anything at all. But this makes no difference. It is the opening of the door that counts, and the sober truth is that we usually need the help of someone else to get the door open. Seldom do we carry the keys to our own prisons! We are frighteningly dependent upon others, but what is more frightening is that others are equally dependent upon us. If we are faithless, there is no second way.

Thus the redemptive society turns out to be, in an almost shocking sense, a responsible society. We are responsible because we are really free, and our freedom includes the frightful privilege of horrible failure which may affect the welfare of innocent men and women whom God loves, but who may not really know His love apart from our own inadequate ministry. The words of Christ, then, apply to all of the ordinary members of the modest yet amazing society to which Christ gave His thought, His effort, His teaching, and His love. The keys are carried today by every man and woman who, in spite of unworthiness, belongs sincerely to this fellowship which is still liberating the world.

CONVERSION WITHIN THE CHURCH

Unless one is born anew, he cannot see the kingdom of God. JOHN 3:3

All who care about the spiritual life of our country are bound to be interested in the announcement of the findings of a nation-wide religious census. There was general expectation that the census would indicate a claim of religious affiliation on the part of the majority of citizens, but few were prepared for the extreme nature of the results. The really striking feature is the fact that nearly all of the people of the United States claim to be church people. Only 4 per cent of those who are fourteen years of age or older deny all church connection. Ninty-six per cent claim to have a membership or to have been baptized or to have some real affiliation with a church or synagogue.

Superficially this is good news, but if we look at it a little more thoroughly, it is very disturbing. What is disturbing is the realization of how trivial the connection must be for millions of those thus reporting. We know very well that, for many of them, there is no deep commitment to the cause of Christ, no regularity of attendance at public worship, no sacrificial giving, no personal religious discipline. If the aim is to get people's names on lists of members, we seem to have been remarkably successful, but the success is often wholly lacking in deeper meaning.

50

Almost every local church is happy to announce, particularly at Easter, large accessions to the membership, and all are encouraged when this represents genuine new life. But an examination of the figures shows, in many instances, that the apparent gain is merely a trading of members between churches. Many are transfers. If we eliminate the transfers, and the children we should expect to gain anyway, the remaining number—those who come as adults into membership by conviction, with no previous connection—is small indeed.

In all honesty we have to say that there are many churches going along today with apparent success, but with real failure, because the new births within the membership are so rare. It is relatively easy today to carry on a successful church with little or no new life. It is not really very hard to raise enough money to build impressive buildings, because money has, in the recent past, been abundant. In fact it is easier to build a building than it is to keep the promise implied in accepting the gifts for the building fund. It is far easier to set up brick walls than to stir up new life in members. Likewise it is easier to get a crowd than it is to secure real conversions.

Important as are concepts such as the lay ministry and the small redemptive groups, there are untold millions in the church today who go forward wholly untouched by these revolutionary ideas. They take their children to Sunday School, go home to read the Sunday paper, and then drive the car back to get the children. A recent cover cartoon of *The New Yorker* brought chills to any sensitive observer, when it showed fathers in their cars, lined up outside a church building, waiting for Sunday School to end. The disturbing fact is that most of the men would undoubtedly list themselves, in any census, as being affiliated with the church outside which they patiently wait each week.

51

Many of those who park their cars and do go in have a relationship to the church which is almost as marginal as that of the waiting fathers. They attend rather often, they think, but of course they do so only when attendance is convenient. They decide each Sunday morning whether they will share in public worship that day—an odd decision on the part of a person who is a recruit in Christ's Cause! When they get there, they normally take seats as far back in the sanctuary as can be found. Instead of merely deploring this situation the path of wisdom is to recognize it clearly and to develop our strategy accordingly. If our only mission field is that of the 4 per cent who claim no affiliation, our opportunities for religious advance are severely limited. But the unattached do not constitute our sole or even our main mission field. Our main mission field today, so far as America is concerned, is within the church membership itself.

The 4 per cent who admit that they are wholly outside any church are, of course, important and must be reached, if possible. Some of them may be potentially strong Christians like Bishop Pike of Grace Cathedral in San Francisco. When Bishop Pike and his wife were married they were so antagonistic to the church that they deliberately had a purely secular ceremony. The bishop, then a lawyer, had been trained in the Roman Catholic Church, had revolted against it, and considered himself as having no religious affiliation at all. His conversion to a vital Christianity was a tremendous gain, and one which we should always seek to duplicate. But we must not be satisfied with aiming merely for the minority. What is far more hopeful is strategy in which we aim deliberately for the millions who think they need no conversion because they have some kind of marginal membership already.

What is important to understand is the nature of the

penalty if we fail to employ such a strategy. If a mild and uncommitted faith becomes standard, the result is utter failure, even if we build expensive church buildings and occasionally have big crowds. The religion of easy demands leads directly to a future in which the power of the gospel is almost wholly lost. If we do not undertake the proper action in time our faith in the Western world will become as meaningless as was the religion of Rome in the last days of the empire. The appearances continued, but the life was gone.

The task before us is clear. The task is to try to reach the present membership of churches with a message of such vitality that they experience a conversion within the church, rather than a conversion to the church. For a man to call himself a member today may mean very little, for it is unfashionable to be outside the church. But, meaningless as membership may be, it has one enormous advantage: it makes a person vulnerable to a deeper appeal. Members are those whom we have a right to try to reach.

The movement from nominal Christianity to a committed Christianity is one of the most exciting of our age. There is no way of having a census report on how many such men and women now exist, and there never will be, but there is no mistaking the reality when we see it. What is remarkable, in almost every case, is the size of the change which occurs. The step taken is a big one; the change is revolutionary. This is because the difference between mild religion and a vital Christianity is not a difference in degree, but a difference in kind.

A vivid illustration of conversion within the church is that of a doctor of medicine in an Oregon city. When this doctor came out of the war and started his practice, he considered his religious affiliation and decided to follow the conventional pattern. He knew exactly what to do. He was, like almost everyone else, a church member and this he proposed to remain. After all, it is bad form not to be a member; it is faintly un-American. He did not expect to take his church membership seriously. The matter of attendance, he thought, he would leave to his wife and children. And, of course, he would make a token contribution. This pattern will be sadly familiar to many.

Something happened in the doctor's mind to make the continuation of this mild pattern impossible. He did some reading of current Christian books which began to arouse him out of his complacency about the church. He met a singularly wise pastor. As a consequence he realized that the church does not exist to provide cheap baby sitting on Sundays, but is intended to be a movement which shakes the world. In any case, the message began to shake him. The result is that, today, this doctor is one of the strong exponents of lay ministry in his own community and is working hard at the job. He has helped to establish an unusually vital prayer group and he shares in a marriage clinic in order to apply the principles of the gospel to one of the most serious problems of modern civilization, the problem of broken homes. In all this, the doctor is finding wonderful joy.

The point of this story is that the big change came within the life of one who was already a member. If there had been a religious census ten years ago, this man would have been counted as part of the large percentage claiming church affiliation, but the counting would have meant almost nothing. All that church affiliation meant for the doctor was that he was thereby laid open to the possibility of conversion. His mild affiliation was important, not in itself, but in what it made possible. It put him in a position to be influenced; it made him open to conviction through the printed word.

Membership is highly ambiguous in meaning, but at least it means opportunity.

Those who are taking advantage of the opportunity and are thus demonstrating a genuine reformation within the church represent not a mass movement, but something which may rightly be called a movement in depth. This movement is curiously independent of denominations in that it can be found, in a similar fashion, in all. Wherever it occurs it is not so much a matter of numbers as of the quality of the commitment. Thus it makes little difference whether we are referring to what is taking place in an Episcopal church of Baltimore, a Lutheran church of Lancaster, a Presbyterian church of Sacramento, or a church in Washington which has no denominational label at all. Similar events are occurring in each. So much has the meaning of membership changed for these churches that one of them, the church in Lancaster, has refused eight hundred applications for membership in five years. The church refused the memberships because of evidence that those making the applications were not seriously intending to become fellow workers in Christ's cause, but were, instead, seeking prestige or respectability. At the same time this church has adopted a standard of giving which requires that the amount annually allotted to the expenses of the local church should always be equaled or surpassed by the amount given to others.

Encouraging examples of conversion within the church may be found in various countries, two of the most heartening being in Great Britain. One of these is in an old parish church belonging to the Church of England, St. Martin's of Birmingham. There the old church at the heart of a great industrial city is coming alive, and the chief evidence of life is to be seen in the new acceptance of responsibility on the part of mature men and women in secular callings. The whole church membership is making a revolutionary change in that there is general acceptance of the discipline of giving one-tenth of all expendable income. One has to know how little responsibility is often accepted by members of an established church, supported by endowments, to know what a revolutionary change the Birmingham experiment represents. One hundred and thirty men and women are organized, in teams of two each, to reach their fellow members with an appeal to the kind of commitment which the team members already accept.

An equally striking experiment is that being conducted in St. George's Tron Church in Glasgow. Only a few years ago it was expected that the old church building, in the heart of the business district of Glasgow, would be demolished, for its days of vitality seemed to be over. Now, however, the church is bursting at the seams, is planning a new social center, and is ministering to the needs of a city population in highly imaginative ways. The chief change that has come is the change in the lives of the members, who are now giving great blocks of time to the effort to reach those who have not been reached before. Instead of giving over Saturday night to wordly interests, the members now conduct a youth rally on the first Saturday night of each month, with an average attendance of one thousand. On Friday nights they go in teams to the coffee bars on the city streets, conduct street meetings, and draw the derelicts back to the church buildings. Some of the members now spend all of each Friday night in this intense ministry to the broken. The consequence has been remarkable changes, some of the present members of the choir being ex-convicts. The major changes have come as the members have been aroused to new understandings of what enlistment in Christ's cause can mean. It may be freely admitted that the available illustrations of this theme are all too few, but the fact that there are any is our basis of hope.

It must be made clear that the crucial change envisioned in this new "inside evangelism" is not one that is marked merely by busywork about the church. The conversion is not real or adequate when it involves merely some work on committees and no more. It is, unfortunately, possible to accept responsibility in a church and yet not be involved in any spiritual life deeper than that normally found in a business or a service club. This is not what we mean. The conversion which is so thrillingly possible is that in which a marginal member may become, not merely a person of ecclesiastical activity, but one who learns to pray, to study, and to think creatively about the Christian cause.

In several churches today leading members are giving many hours to church work, but they do not grow personally because they are dealing with practically nothing but money. Of course the budget must be raised, and the buildings built, but these do not touch the heart of the matter. The church was before the building was constructed, and we hope it will continue to be after the building is destroyed. A man can work on a building committee and miss the goal, for the goal is the full entrance into partnership with Christ in prayer and in personal evangelism. The physical facilities must be seen as mere tools, useful only insofar as they contribute to an end. The end is the complete losing of ourselves in the love of God.

Unfortunately a man can serve as an usher and yet not feel the spirit of worship. Indeed his very ushering is some· times a hindrance to the reality of worship. Some go out to count the money while others stay to pray. Even men in the ministry may find it difficult to pass beyond the mechanics to the reality. They are so taken up with the management of worship that they fail to worship. A great deal of what is ordinarily called church work may itself be an escape from God and His demands on a person's life.

At first sight it seems paradoxical to say that the mission field is in the church, but the more we think of it, the more we see that this accords with common sense. It was ever thus. Who were the people who were first touched by Christ's message? Were they the counterpart of our residents of Skid Row? Of course not! They were persons who were already religious, though sometimes in a purely conventional sense. But this was the means by which they were drawn over. Look at Nicodemus who came to Jesus by night. It was to him that Jesus said, "You must be born again." He wasn't a murderer; he wasn't a criminal; he wasn't a pagan; he wasn't an atheist; he wasn't an outsider. What Christ is saying to everyone, then, in the third chapter of John, is that the new birth must come even to the insiders; it must come to people like ourselves.

In the Billy Graham Crusade in New York there were certain skeptics who sometimes complained that the figures were not dependable because, they said, many of the persons who made decisions for Christ were already church members. Therefore, they said, the statistical reports were not accurate. What amazing misunderstanding this shows on the part of the critic! It is true that a number of those who made their public decision came out of the great massed choir, made up of members of the choirs of New York churches. But why should that be surprising? Again, the problem is that of Nicodemus. Is it self-evident that, because a person had been singing in a choir, he therefore did not need new life? It would be absurd to say this. Of course many of the converts came out of the churches. From where else could they come, in a society in which most people claim to be church people already?

The theme of conversion within the church is as old as Christianity and older. It is, indeed, the theme of the most admired parable of the Old Testament, Ezekiel's parable of the Valley of Dry Bones. The parable pictures Israel as dried up and nearly lost, with no evidence of life. All that remains is the bones, with all flesh and with all vitality lacking. The point to remember is that the deadness which the prophet pictures is not that of the pagan peoples, but of God's chosen ones. The excitement of the parable lies in the conviction that however dry the bones are, new life within them is always possible. The miracle of regeneration can occur; the church can be revived on the inside. Perhaps the most moving line of the story is "Breathe on these slain that they may live." And the wonder is that Ezekiel's prophecy has been justified by events in many succeeding generations. Reformation occurs and it occurs repeatedly. Though Ezekiel was talking about Israel, his parable applies equally well to the Church of Christ as the New Israel. God's interest is not merely in reaching outsiders, important as they are; He is concerned equally with changing the insiders.

As we face the future we are inspired by a great and yet reasonable hope. It is the hope that the sort of thing that occurred in the life of the Oregon doctor can occur in the lives of people in every church and in every community. It is the existence of such people, with their marvelous potentiality, which can never let us rest, once we understand the difference that can be made. The unharvested harvest is one of the most disturbing ideas that can enter the human mind.

CALLED TO BE SAINTS

Paul, called by the will of God to be an apostle of Christ Jesus, and our brother Sosthenes, to the church of God which is at Corinth, to those consecrated in Christ Jesus, called to be saints. I CORINTHIANS 1:1, 2

Are you a saint? It is not necessary to wait for an answer to this question, for it is wholly predictable. No matter how deeply steeped in the Christian faith the person thus questioned happens to be, his answer, in the great majority of cases, will be a flat negative. And his firm denial of sainthood will, almost inevitably, be accompanied by a smile. The very idea that John Brown or Mary Smith of the Second Baptist Church of Jonesboro should be considered a saint is preposterous and laughable.

The near universality of this answer is surprising, in view of the fact that saint is the standard term used to denote an ordinary Christian in the New Testament. Read the introductory verses of the great Epistles and see what you find. The profoundly theological book of Romans is not addressed just to leaders or to theological students, but to the rank and file of Roman Christians, "To all God's beloved in Rome, called to be saints." Both of the Corinthian letters are similarly addressed, the group mentioned in the second letter being the more widespread of the two: "To the church of God which is at Corinth, with all the saints who are in the whole of Achaia." Ephesians casts the widest net of all, being unlimited by geography: "To the saints who are also faithful in Christ Jesus." The deeply affectionate letter called Philippians is addressed "To all the saints in Christ Jesus who are at Philippi, with the bishops and deacons." This is a vivid and unmisakable way of making the point clear that sainthood is not meant to be limited to appointed leaders. In early Christianity, saint and member were merely synonymous terms.

In view of this standard use in New Testament Christianity, it is hard to understand our present reluctance to employ such an attractive term as saint when applied to ourselves. If it was suitable for Aquila and Priscilla, why is it not suitable for John and Mary? In answer we may say that most contemporary Christians do not realize, when they reject the term saint, that they are likewise rejecting early Christian practice. Perhaps most of them have not read, with any care, the opening verses of the epistles and, even if they have done so, they tend to think of the ancient vocabulary as being almost entirely irrelevant to our life today. Furthermore, all of us are the victims of a decline in language. During the last few hundred years the word saint has slowly come to mean something radically different from what it meant in Corinth and Ephesus, when the church of Jesus Christ was young. Now, in common parlance, the word saint tends to refer to someone who has been canonized. It means, normally, a person who lived a long time ago and who performed authentic miracles. Sometimes it is required for canonization that the person should have been affiiliated with one particular church.

What is important for us to understand, as fully as we can, is that the meaning of saint which has grown up in subsequent years is a departure from the Biblical conception, and is in no way an improvement. It is really far more helpful to think of a saint as one who may be alive today and very modest in his evidences of virtue. Indeed, sainthood in the New Testament sense, which should again be our sense, is compatible with a good deal of human failure. Therefore, the person who counters the question whether he is a saint, by the stock answer, "No, I am a sinner," is demonstrating a fundamental confusion about the Christan situation. In the original meaning, saint and sinner, far from being incompatible terms, were terms applicable to the same people. Certainly we know that many of the recipients of the Letters to Young Churches were sinners to a serious degree, but this did not keep them from being called saints. They were saints, not because of their virtue, but because of their calling, for the truth is that extremely inadequate people can be called. "God chose what is low and despised in the world, even things that are not, to bring to nothing things that are."

Christianity abounds in paradoxes, but the central paradox is that of the very nature of the church. In order to tell the truth about the church it is always necessary to say, not merely one thing, but at least two. We must tell about the glory of the church and we must tell about its degradation, and we must tell of both at once. If we tell only of the glory we become hopelessly romantic, but if we tell only of the degradation we lose heart. In actual practice the church includes the best and the worst and often they appear in close proximity.

On the one hand it is part of the authentic record that the church has been the most creative single force in modern culture. The church has been the mother of the arts, the founder of colleges, and thus, directly, the encouragement of science, the builder of hospitals, the inspiration of democracy. For generations the strongest voices raised against slavery and war and racial injustice have been voices originating within the bosom of the church. All of this is on the record and it is deeply encouraging.

On the other hand, the church has been divided and divisive and it has developed its own forms of the struggle for prestige and power. Often, in its buildings, the church is trying consciously to impress the world by purchasing sites on the highest hills and engaging in vulgar display. Sometimes the church is behind the world on social issues and, even though it provides the leaders in the struggle for racial justice, it likewise provides, in some places, the last refuge for those who believe in white supremacy. Though the church annually gives millions of dollars for foreign missions, seeking unselfishly to lift the lives of persons whom the givers have never seen and never will see, sometimes this very generosity does harm by the perpetuation of sectarian divisions and rivalries in foreign areas where they are truly disastrous. Sometimes the American church is more interested in Negroes in Africa than it is in Negroes in Detroit.

It is this moral complexity that has marked the saints from the beginning. Nowhere is this more evident than in the situation represented by the First Letter to the Corinthians, the beginning of which provides a text for this sermon. In some ways the saints at Corinth were the most fortunate people imaginable. In any case they received the finest letter ever written.

Most thoughtful persons, if they were asked to name the very best literary production of the whole world, might at first consider mentioning the Homeric poems, or part of the *Divine Comedy*, or one of the sonnets or other writings of Shakespeare or even one of Milton's sonnets, such as that on his blindness. But it is a common experience for such people, when they have thought still more carefully, to fasten upon the remarkable production of that strangely gifted man, Paul of Tarsus, which begins, "If I speak in the tongues of men and of angels, but have not love, I am a noisy gong or a clanging cymbal." All, of every faith and every tongue, are moved when they reach the climax and read, "Love is patient and kind; love is not jealous or boastful; it is not arrogant or rude. Love does not insist on its own way." These words, as any person can understand, reflect authentic greatness. We bow before them in admiration and in humility. We cannot write like that! We do not know how Paul accomplished the feat, particularly when we accept the overt evidence that the letter was actually dictated. This we know because of the postscript in Paul's own hand. Our general judgment today is that the best literature is not produced by dictation, but perhaps we are wrong.

Thrilled as we are with Paul's magnificent poem on love, we seldom stop to consider the situation which called it forth. Was it written because the Corinthian saints were so loving? Assuredly not. It was written because they were so lacking in love. When we examine the letter to the saints carefully, we are almost embarrassed by what we find. The church members to whom the world's best words were written were guilty of all kinds of sins. In the first place the Athenian Christian community, tiny as it was, was already divided into competing cliques. "It has been reported to me by Chloe's people," Paul says, "that there is quarreling among you." Four competing factions are named. Later, it is mentioned that some are openly arrogant and boastful. Still worse, "It is actually reported that there is immorality among you, of a kind that is not found even among pagans" (I Cor. 5:1). Many had grievances with one another, some so great that they instituted lawsuits against other saints. There is a frank reference to prostitution. Perhaps the most surprising complaint of all, however, is that of a failure of love in the celebration of the love feast or the Lord's Supper. The complaint was that "in eating, each one goes ahead with his own meal, and one is hungry and another is drunk" (I Cor. 11:21).

What was meant to be uniting became divisive, because, in the absence of sharing, the contrasts of wealth and poverty became even more glaring. The effect of the show put on by the rich was the humiliation of those who had little or nothing.

It is only when this list of sins of the saints is kept in mind that the true meaning of the greatest chapter becomes clear. It was because the saints were arrogant and rude that Paul said that love "is not arrogant or rude." In short, the worst illuminates the best and the best illuminates the worst. The highest and the lowest are close together in something of the fashion of Mt. Whitney and Death Valley.

These references to the Corinthians of the first century help us to understand the idea of sainthood, for we are still like them in both their glory and their shame. A saint may be a sinner, but he is a sinner who is called to a redemptive task. The calling is of such a nature that it makes people more than themselves. Humble as they are, and unworthy as they are, saints are ordinary men and women who are called to be Christ's ambassadors in contemporary common life. This is what determines the meaning of the church, which is not for people who think they are good, but for people who, knowing that they are not good, are nevertheless trying to respond to a call to represent Christ in their daily experiences. The church is the *ecclesia*, the society of the called out. We are not asked to leave the world in order to retreat to some little separated Christian community, but to make our witness in the midst of the mixture.

The greatest call which comes today to church members who are willing to try to be contemporary saints is a call to demonstration. It is our responsibility to show to the world a better Christian society than any which has been known. The point is that one demonstration carries more weight than many words. This is why the experiment carried on since the autumn of 1947 by the Church of the Saviour in Washington D.C. has seemed so important to so many people who care greatly about the impact of Christ's church upon the world.

When Gordon and Mary Cosby planned their lives after the war, they took plenty of time to consider the future. Because Gordon Cosby was a brilliant speaker and a skillful organizer, he could easily have entered an ordinary pastorate and would probably have made an outstanding success. It would not have been hard for him to find, on leaving the chaplaincy, a pastorate in which he would minister to more than a thousand members. But the Cosbys decided, after careful deliberation, to turn their backs upon this attractive and worthwhile prospect. Instead, they wanted to make a radical demonstration of what a truly committed church might be. They had nothing but admiration for what other pastors were doing in the established churches, but it was increasingly clear to them that God was calling them to a peculiar task. They felt that their chief call was the call to demonstrate.

The consequences of this decision in 1947 have been far-reaching. Today the laboratory church that was set up is still small; it still makes use of modest facilities; it still seeks to be loyal to its peculiar task. Today it has a membership of 59 with an annual budget of $59,000 and no members who are wealthy. The giving of both time and money is costly, but glorious. The level of commitment is high, the ministry to others is expected, and the affection is infectious. Anyone who comes into close contact with the experiment is bound to be glad that Gordon Cosby made his decision as he did. If he were today serving a big church, he would influence hundreds, but by serving a little church he is influencing thousands. Members of all kinds of churches in various parts of the world have been so challenged by the story, as it has appeared in both the secular and the religious press, that their own sights have been raised.

The paradox of smallness, which the Church of the Saviour demonstrates, is one which goes deeply into all of Christian experience. We are not called to be big; we are not called to ape worldly standards; we are not called to succeed. We are called, instead, to make the kind of demonstration which can challenge the world and all of the people in it. We are called to do something different from the world, for the sake of the world.

Though this pattern is clear, it leaves unsolved the problem of the person who seriously wishes to accept the responsibilities of humble sainthood, but who has no fellowship like that of the Church of the Saviour with which he can join. The more or less conventional denominational church in his neighborhood has a good building, and a good many members, but it is certainly not the sort of fellowship which excites people when they read about it or come into first contact with it. What should the would-be saint do about his church membership in these highly familiar circumstances?

All of us really know the answer already. Most of us are called to try to make the demonstration where we are, even if it is not a striking one. The call of the Corinthians was to work in the poor Corinthian church, even though it was rent by discord. However glad Gordon Cosby is that he made his decision as he did, he is not urging others to try to do the same. Perhaps one such demonstration is enough. It suffices to make the challenge felt; it raises the standard; it shows what reality in membership may mean. But most of the saints in Youngstown or Waterloo are called to do something else. They are called to try to bring into their established and diffused churches as much of reality in membership, as much of sacrificial giving, as much of unlimited liabilty for one another as can be produced in such a setting. They cannot overcome entirely the handicap inherent in the fact that many of the so-called members are inactive or absentees or unconcerned, but they can learn how to minister to the people in these classifications.

It is especially important that the saints should not be so infected with the virus of perfectionism that they refuse to work in the lukewarm churches where their responsibilities naturally fall. There is a type of man, painfully familiar, who refuses to work in the inadequate church in his community because his ideal of what a church ought to be is so high that he cannot bear the actual compromise which faces him. Such a person is missing his one chance to make a real difference. If we wait for perfection we shall still be waiting when we come to the end of our days. However bad the existing local church is, the alternative of a churchless society is certainly worse. This is vividly apparent when we note the self-righteousness of the outside critics of the church, which is so much worse than anything we know on the inside. The man who cannot join the church because he is too virtuous for it is really in a bad predicament. He has all of the sins of the saints with the added difficulty that he does not have, as they do, constant reminders of his own unworthiness. He is not part of a society of the broken who are united in the recognition that they *are* broken. He does not share in a repeated service which puts a high priority upon penitence and prayer for forgiveness. The church, as has often been said, is like the ark during the flood. We could not stand the confusion inside were it not for the storm outside.

We are called, as saints, to be in the churches that now

exist and to try to change their character, beginning with ourselves. The method of change is to build the church within the church, but to do so with humility and not with pride. The solution of the problem of pride is to hold the standard of Christ so constantly before our eyes that our own little achievements are bound to appear as poor as they really are. The persons who are most thoroughly part of the fellowship of the concerned tend also to be the most truly humble. They are humble, not because they think badly of themselves, but because their concern for the Christian cause is so intense that they forget to think about themselves at all.

The church within the church is not called to be different in a few queer customs, such as dress or adornment, but different in the quality of commitment. We are called to be a peculiar people, but we must reserve our peculiarities for the big issues. Those who try to be peculiar in trivial details are not listened to in great matters because their witness is discounted from the first.

We are a long way from knowing all that is involved in the call of Christ, which constitutes the only sainthood we know, but we soon discover that as we try faithfully to obey the simple calls we hear, the ability to hear seems to grow. We are well on the road when at last we are willing to admit, without self-consciousness, that sainthood is our goal.

THE
COURAGE
TO
CARE

Most men's love will grow cold. MATT. 24:12

Nothing is stranger in contemporary life than our fear of emotion. And one of the strangest features of this fear is its inconsistency. We are, for example, irrationally afraid of emotion in our religion, but we habitually give way to something like frenzy at basketball games. Our greatest fear of emotion is always found in areas of deep meaning and conviction. We are a little ashamed to show any depth of feeling in connection with patriotism and we are even more ashamed to show it in connection with our faith. Thus there are many who would resent it bitterly if doubt were cast upon their sincerity as Christians, but who, nevertheless, feel self-conscious and reticent about singing "Jesus, Lover of My Soul" or some other gospel song which expresses deep feeling. The idea is that we are not intellectually respectable unless we keep cool. Other and lesser men may be deeply moved, but it is our privilege to stay above the battle of emotionally held convictions. Even the free way of life is something which is quite all right, but certainly not something to get hot and bothered about. We hate Marxism, but we are singularly reticent about the efforts to develop or adopt an alternative creed to which we can give ourselves enthusiastically. Students are terribly shy of school loyalty and are increasingly

70

self-conscious while singing *Alma Mater*. Strong enthusiasm is frowned upon among "organization men" of all generations. Such fear is even reflected in our popular language. How else can we explain the fact that the word "cool" is, in our current jargon, a word of approbation?

One of the best ways to overcome the popular fear of emotion is to try to understand the reason for it. When we begin the examination seriously the answer is abundantly clear. We are afraid to exhibit emotion because we are afraid of appearing ridiculous. Man is so made that he hates terribly to be the object of laughter. He can face antagonism or fierce hatred with magnificent courage, but laughter is much harder to face. Now it is perfectly clear that everyone who shows emotion about some cause, or even about some person, living or dead, runs a serious risk of seeming to be foolish. The cause may not succeed; the person may turn out to be less perfect than the admirer supposed; the ideal espoused may cease to be popular.

In the light of such danger anyone can figure out where the path of safety lies. Safety lies in not going out on a limb; it lies in staying coolly aloof; it lies in carefully maintained detachment. This path of detachment is so plain and so clearly marked that it has led to the development of something like a cult. The members of the cult are marked everywhere by the unwillingness to take a strong position of either approval or disapproval. Let us say that we are looking at a new painting or listening to a new poem. Warmhearted people may react with natural enthusiasm or possibly disgust, but this the person who is carefully cool cannot afford to do. His plan is to play it safe. Accordingly, his response is that the object in question is interesting or, in extreme cases, amusing. One who sticks to this level of response has not said anything of importance, of course, but he has the enormous advantage that he is not likely to be proved wrong.

There are a good many professors in our universities who play this game and play it with great skill. They present ideas, but they do not espouse them. Platonism, Pragmatism, Christianity—all are presented in complete emotional detachment, much as would be done if the objects in question were different numerical systems. And this is done, in spite of the fact that the ideas presented are matters of the highest significance for the human race. Propositions about reality are either true or false, if they are meaningful, but this painful fact is often skillfully avoided. It is easier to present ideas of God than to make a balanced judgment of relevant evidence about the truth of God's objective reality. Most difficult of all is a personal witness concerning conviction. Often the students have no way of knowing what the professor's own position is, for adherence to the cult of detachment will not permit him to reveal this intimate fact. Sometimes he is actually so impressed by a particular conception of the nature of scientific method that he thinks that espousal of any view, or involvement in any faith, would incapacitate him for his scholarly task. If he were more thorough, however, he would know better. He would become alert to the fallacy of *misplaced detachment,* realizing that the mood appropriate to the study of an atom may not be at all appropriate in the study of a man. The cult of detachment is one result of the growth of scientism in our age, a growth which is shown in its extreme form in Russia, but is by no means limited to that country. No doubt it will pass, but for the present it does harm, even in our religious experience.

It is a healthy sign that the fear of emotion is beginning to be challenged and challenged by the very people among whom the fear has been most widespread and damaging. Listen, for example, to a letter written recently by a high

school girl in a great American city. The letter was an un-
solicited response to a sermon which she heard.

I have been thinking much this year about the importance of
caring, of passion in life. I have often realized that it takes courage
to care. Caring is dangerous; it leaves you open to hurt and to
looking a fool; and perhaps it is because they have been hurt so
often that people are afraid to care. You can't die if you are not
alive, but then who would rather be a stone?

I have found many places in my own life where I keep a secret
store of indifference as a sort of self-protection, but I have been
trying instead to feel the wholeness of the part and not shut my-
self to life and still to keep a perspective of the eternal and infinite potential, which prevents the inevitable disappointments in
some parts from becoming a disappointment or fear of all of life.
It is a hard thing and I have often failed. Sensitivity, or caring, is
its own reward.

Caring is like the love T. S. Eliot speaks of in his *Four Quarters*:

> *Desire itself is movement*
> *Not in itself desirable;*
> *Love is itself unmoving,*
> *Only the cause and end of movement,*
> *Timeless, and undesiring*
> *Except in the aspect of time*
> *Caught in the form of limitation*
> *Between un-being and being.*[1]

In this last aspect, common to all of us, we cannot help but
desire; yet I feel that desire not based on love cannot end in other
than frustration.

Sincerely,
Jane

When we remember that this was written by a high school
girl, we recognize that it indicates a truly penetrating in-

[1] From "Burnt Norton" in *Four Quartets*, copyright, 1943, by T. S. Eliot.
Reprinted by permission of Harcourt, Brace and Company, Inc., and Faber
and Faber.

sight. Notice her reference to "a secret store of indifference." She understands perfectly that, apart from the fear of ridicule, caring would be admitted by all of us. If you are passionate, she tells you, you are vulnerable; you are running the risk that you may be hurt. If you love another person with all your heart, you can be hurt far more by that person than by anybody about whom you do not care. Devotion to a cause puts you in a situation in which you can look ridiculous. What if that about which you are passionate fails? What if your cause is not accomplished? You can look like a fool and do. This then is the advice to give anybody who never wants to be hurt: *don't care!* Don't care and then nobody can ever say, "I told you so." Don't care and you cannot be wounded because of the caring. If you don't want to be hurt, don't marry, and then you can't lose. If you never want to be hurt, don't have a child. A child whom you love so much could be a terrible disappointment. If you never want to be hurt, don't enter the church. Even this redemptive fellowship, on which Christ depends, can itself be disappointing and manifestly unworthy. Don't care and then you will be safe.

You can, if you wish, develop a hard, glittering exterior, never involved, never personally concerned, and then nobody can ever chide you for having gone out on a limb. Nobody, then, can ever truthfully say that the idea that you have espoused has turned out to be false, because you have never espoused any. But those who take this road to safety pay a heavy price, the price of turning their backs upon all of the best things in life.

The important thing to say now is that cool detachment is the exact antithesis of the Gospel of Jesus Christ. Christ calls us into a kind of life in which we can be wounded. You cannot look at the Cross in detachment; you have to carry it yourself and you have to carry it in your own heart. Caring

74

is, indeed, dangerous, but it is essential to Christian discipleship. One of the greatest contributions which the gospel
can make to our confused age is that it may be the very
means by which men and women can overcome their crip-
pling fear of emotion. The gospel is highly relevant to our
time if it can help to produce the courage to care.

The Christian emphasis in this direction now has assistance
from a somewhat surprising quarter in the general existen-
tialist analysis of the knowing situation. What the main
stream of existentialism has taught is that, in important
matters, there is no true insight without involvement. Every
man knows things about himself which no one else knows,
even though others may understand some things about him
to which he may be blind. But the outsider never knows, if
he remains merely an outsider. If he is to understand, he
must put himself metaphorically into the other person's
shoes.

There is a tiny grain of truth in the old saw that love is
blind, but in most respects the adage is false. The man who
loves is aware of aspects of the personality of the beloved
which are entirely hidden to those who hate and largely
hidden to those who do not care. Caring heightens the sensitivity and sharpens the vision. It was only in their passionate attachment that Simon Peter and the other Apostles
began to understand who Jesus really was. Out of His affection the unstable Simon was able to see that Jesus was indeed
the Christ, the Son of the Living God. This insight did not
come to those who stood off in splendid detachment or who
were mere curious observers. And the revelation did not
come to the Apostles at first; it came to them only after they
had experienced personal involvement in Christ's cause.
Very little is revealed, in any area, to those who are not so
involved that they have a stake in the outcome of events.

It is probable that even a system like that of Leninism is not really understood by those who have not shared in its misguided demand for commitment.

Long before existentialism was originated, Christianity maintained that insight through involvement was the only method by which real understanding is ever possible. Christ's first words to disciples were concerned not with belief, but with participation in a movement. The gospel begins and ends on the note, "Follow me." The last chapter of the last gospel represents the risen Christ as saying, in response to Peter's question about another, "What is that to thee? Follow thou me." The secret of understanding according to the Letter to the Ephesians is of a similar nature. Love is presented, not as a deterrent to knowledge, but as the very organ of knowledge. "That you, being rooted and grounded in love, may have power to *comprehend*" is one important way of stating a whole theory of knowledge. Often, in subsequent developments of Christian literature, the same note has been struck. The best-known example is in the widely loved hymn, "Jesus, the Very Thought of Thee," in which the crucial lines read:

> *The love of Jesus what it is*
> *None but His loved ones know.*

The outside observer cannot expect to perceive with any adequacy, because he has not met the conditions of insight. That there are also dangers of self-delusion in this approach anyone can see, but the part of wisdom is to face these dangers boldly by combining both involvement and a high degree of intellectual honesty. The point to remember is that the intellectual honesty, without the courage to care, is bound to end in intellectual and spiritual sterility.

What it a Christian? A Christian is a person who has fallen

in love with Jesus Christ and who is, consequently, willing to witness to that love and to try to demonstrate it, as Christ's emissary, to all the rest of God's children. It is not cold detachment. It is not looking at the gospel and saying, "That is an interesting idea." Such an approach, whatever the field of inquiry, doesn't get us anywhere at all. Life is a great mystery at best; it is the sort of thing that is never penetrated apart from passion. A Christian is one who looks at the life of Christ and who is so moved by it that he says, "I love Thee, Lord Jesus. Come into my heart; come in today; come in to stay."

One cannot study many pages of the New Testament without a keen realizaton of the passionate character of early Christianity. This is shown, at white heat, in the recorded experiences of those who entered the fellowship immediately after the first Pentecost. In one day, according to the Book of Acts, there were added three thousand souls.

And they devoted themselves to the apostles' teaching and fellowship, to the breaking of bread and prayers. And fear came upon every soul; and many wonders and signs were done through the apostles. And all who believed were together and had all things in common; and they sold their possessions and goods and distributed them to all, as any had need. And day by day, attending the temple together and breaking bread in their homes, they partook of food with glad and generous hearts.

Such a passage assists us greatly in our effort to understand how original Christianity was able to endure and to win against such odds as existed. It involved study, and fellowship, and unlimited liability for one another, and prayer and reverence and joy. There is, therefore, really no mystery about the endurance of the movement. Theirs was a fellowship of the concerned, a society of those who cared and who were not ashamed to care.

There are some people who think that this kind of religion is unsuitable for modern intellectuals, even though they admit that it was the New Testament pattern. They think that this is the kind of religion found only in the fringe groups. But this is where they are wrong. The greatest of the intellectuals, like Kierkegaard, are the ones who have seen most clearly that life without passion is no life at all. The sober truth is that there is no new life without passion. No baby was ever conceived without passion; no great poem was ever produced without passion; no great piece of music was ever composed without passion. Passion is what takes us beyond the superficiality of life to a deep and wonderful glow in which we learn to care.

Most people go through a phase in which they are ashamed to show any genuine emotion in relation to their families or in relation to their religion. Some feel a certain hesitancy in singing such a hymn as "When I survey the wondrous cross on which the Prince of Glory died," and they would be terribly embarrassed by a public call to commitment, but often this is only a phase, a kind of extended adolescence. The fact that this is so common, particularly in youth, is what makes the letter from the high school girl so remarkable. What is encouraging is to see evidence that, while pseudo-sophistication may make people fear to express any deep passion, a greater advancement may lead to the complete overcoming of this fear. In this connection it is heartening to read the accounts of how Thornton Wilder, in a sophisticated academic environment, used to gather boys about him on Sunday evening to play and to sing the old gospel songs. He had outgrown his fears, if ever he had any, and could be utterly unself-conscious about the love of Christ. Yet Wilder is bound to be counted among the true intellectuals of this generation. Only one who has outgrown the fear of showing emotion could have used so effectively, in *Our Town,* the singing of "Blest Be the Tie That Binds." The person who can see this and can weep without fear of ridicule has already escaped some of the worst spiritual perils of our age.

The recovery or discovery of the significance of caring may be a really creative feature in contemporary thought. In part it comes from the study of the works of Martin Heidegger, but this is not the only source. A prominent philosopher of England has suggested the wisdom of using "caring" as our best modern translation for the almost untranslatable Greek word, of which the thirteenth chapter of First Corinthians is an inspired definition. The difficulty with "charity" as a translation is that, to modern ears, it means philanthropy and not much more. The trouble with "love" is that it has been oversentimentalized in modern literature and smacks of softness. But caring is, as yet, an unspoiled term. It is the best we know. Thus we may begin: "Though I speak with the tongues of men and of angels, and *do not care,* I am become as sounding brass, or a tinkling cymbal." "Caring never ends." Try, in the intimacy of your own meditation, to restate that marvelous chapter, substituting "caring" for the key word. The consequence may be that you have a new vision of the truth as you begin to understand what it means to have "the courage to care."

Though it seems hardly necessary to mention it, it may be worth while to say that, however necessary caring is, we can care for the wrong things. This is why we need to develop critical insight at the same time. The point to make, however, is that we do not solve the critical problem by a retreat into detachment. Critical investigation and involvement are wholly compatible. We must be honest, but we do not have to become cold in order to do so.

Love, or caring, is the greatest thing in the world, but the awful truth, as Christ said, is that love can grow cold. This is why we gather for worship week by week. We are trying to keep our love warm. We are trying not to lose it. How wonderful if we can keep the glow! What a glorious thing it is to see a man and woman married to each other for years and, instead of settling down into the dull business of living together, they keep the glow and you see their faces light up when they meet in a room. The glory is that their love has not grown cold. It is even more important that this should be true in regard to our love for Christ. Has your love grown cold?

THE VIOLENCE OF THE KINGDOM

The law and the prophets were until John; since them the good news of the kingdom of God is preached, and every one enters it violently. LUKE 16:16.

Two insights, which are both old and new, can illuminate greatly our present understanding of the Christian cause. The first insight is that the conversion which is important is not conversion from sheer paganism to nominal Christianity, not conversion from cold to warm, but conversion from luke-warm to hot, from a mild religion to one in which a person's whole life is taken up and filled and controlled and compelled. The second insight is that the most common situation in which this kind of conversion can occur is the situation of middle-age. Genuine conversion takes place not primarily or chiefly among the young, but much more commonly among men and women who have had some experience of life and who, in their maturity, discover an entirely new conception of what their lives may become.

Many lives might be used to illustrate these two insights at once, but few can illustrate them better than the life of an Ohio lawyer who died in 1957, after long years of emptiness followed by five years of brilliant Christian discipleship. This man had grown up in a church and had attended a Christian college before going to law school, but for years the church connection had meant nothing to him. Christian marriage and Christian baptism were assumed, but Christian discipleship meant nothing at all. He was listed among members, but did not attend or do anything about his religious obligations. During these years, as an increasingly successful lawyer, this man paid no serious attention to the gospel, until, in his forties, he experienced a true conversion, quite as genuine as that of any alleged pagan, although he was never an avowed unbeliever at any time of his life.

The redemptive door by which this man entered Christ's Kingdom was that of Alcoholics Anonymous. He accepted the help of this remarkable fellowship only after he admitted his own helplessness. This occurred when the able man faced his own life with absolute sincerity, about five years before the end of his life. He recognized the fact that, although he was a success in the eyes of the world, in reality he was a failure, his life was a washout, and that he could not handle it. Though his new life began with the helpful fellowship of Alcoholics Anonymous, he found that this was not adequate to his need. Consequently he threw himself into the life of the church, and he threw himself in with all that he had. He found that he believed the gospel; he found that he really accepted the Lordship of Jesus Christ; he found that he was willing to give himself to the kind of life in which he knew nothing but Jesus Christ and Him crucified; and the consequent change was as radical as can be imagined.

From that day he never touched another drop of liquor; he became a marvelous father and husband; he urged his rector to organize a class in the lay ministry to be taught by the rector. He lived to see this class given public recognition in a deeply moving ceremony conducted by his bishop. There were fourteen men in the group, all of whom continue to make a real difference in the life of the church.

This lawyer said, "If I am going to be a Christian, I had better work at it." He immediately changed from nominal giving to giving of more than a tenth of both time and money. He preached almost every Sunday. Whenever opportunity offered he spoke in the boys' home or the old people's home or in any place where there was nobody else to conduct the service. Often he preached in the mental hospital, often in the penitentiary. A common schedule on Sundays included one sermon at 8:00 A.M. in one institution and another at 9:30 in a second, with worship in his own church at 11:00. Frequently he sang with his son in the church choir and, a few times each year, read the Scripture Lesson in the service he loved most. In the last few months of his life, although tired and already stricken with a fatal disease of which he was unaware, he accepted the heavy responsibility of becoming chairman of a campaign for large capital funds for the help of new churches.

Now that he is dead, after such a short time as a Christian, we know that greatness cannot be measured by time. What the man did was to give to the many who loved him a new understanding of what the gospel is. He had to make a big change, or he wouldn't have made any. A little religion wouldn't have helped him a bit. Do you think it would have helped him to leave off just a little of his whiskey and then maybe just add a little to his attendance at church, just add a little to his giving, add a little to his praying, add a little to his public witness? It wouldn't have done anything. There are places in life where, unless you make a big step, you don't really make any step. This is the meaning of conversion.

In the light of the brief but brilliant example of the Christian discipleship of the Ohio lawyer, we can begin to understand some of the words of Jesus that have been highly puzzling. Listen to these: "The law and the prophets," said

Jesus, "were until John. Since then the good news of the Kingdom of God is preached, and every one enters it violently." "Everyone enters it violently." He is saying that if you don't enter it violently, you don't enter it at all. This is very close to the heart of Christ's gospel: the new life, the new start, reborn men and women, a new direction, a new dimension, a new commitment. The big step in life, the commitment, is as truly a crisis as is birth or adolescence or death. Birth is normally a violent occurrence and Christ's affirmation is that a new birth is required.

What do you think Christ means when He says that, if you enter it, you have to enter it violently? It does not necessarily mean suddenly. Birth is not always sudden in either physical birth or spiritual birth. Even in the example we have just described, the change came over a period of two or three months. There wasn't a single day when the lawyer was struck. Yes, the change may indeed be gradual, but the point is that it has to be a radical change in order to be genuine. Our human nature is such that nothing less will suffice. It has to be a change so great that, whether it occurs in a moment or a month or a year, we come out at an utterly different place.

If Christ were speaking to us today, as He spoke earlier to the people of Galilee, and if He were to use parables from contemporary life as He did before, He might easily use the parable of the sonic boom. This He might do, because we know more about jets and their pilots than we know about sheep and their shepherds. The message of the sonic boom is that there is no calm and nonviolent way in which flyers can surpass the speed of sound. The peculiar combination of waves, which occurs at the crucial speed, producing the loud report with which we are increasingly familiar, is something we are not likely to escape or avoid. Some changes are

84

great changes, and what Christ teaches is that Christian discipleship involves such a change. It means entrance into a new kind of experience and organization around a new center.

The chief reason why Christ's phrase about the violence of the Kingdom is puzzling and mystifying to us is that we have, through the years of Christian history, built up an unreal picture of Christ, which we now use as our standard of judgment. We have told ourselves so often of the gentle Jesus, meek and mild, that we are embarrassed by the reality when we have to face it. The actual Christ of history drove the money-changers from the temple and used what can only be called violent language in his verbal chastisement of the Pharisees. His words were powerful and sharp, and if people wanted to be offended, that was their business, for He told the truth.

One phase of the gospel which is embarrassing to all who have constructed the mild stereotype of Christ is that in which He sounds like a revolutionary in His reference to the fire He is trying to set. "I came," He said, "to cast fire upon the earth; and would that it were already kindled! I have a baptism to be baptized with; and how I am constrained until it is accomplished!" (Luke 12:49, 50.) Not even the most ceremonial of Christians would suppose that Christ, in these vivid words, was talking about some physical ceremony to be performed. Perhaps He was thinking of His impending death; perhaps He was thinking of John's prediction that, although he baptized with water, his successor would baptize with fire; perhaps He was thinking of both together. In any case He was shedding new light on His own conception of what the fundamental nature of His enterprise was. He was telling us that the gospel is more explosive than we realize.

In all the great moments of Christian history, vitality has demonstrated itself by the recovery of this burning conviction, this evidence of violence which has nothing whatever to do with physical violence. A good example of such vitality was shown in the middle of the seventeenth century with the emergence of the Quaker movement. So flaming and intense were the convictions of the first Quakers that they were thrown into prison by the thousands and were greatly feared by all who were seeking to preserve the established order. This is the real reason why four were hanged in colonial Boston. Even the intentionally opprobrious nickname "Quaker" was given because the inner disturbance was so great that it sometimes led to actual physical trembling. Though the label was intended as an insult, it was, in fact, highly complimentary in its tacit recognition that these people held their faith in such a manner that they were *shaken* by it. What all observers in Britain and colonial America and even western Europe understood was that these people had entered the Kingdom violently. One of the most vivid of the young men who gathered about George Fox was called by his associates a "Son of Thunder and of Consolation." The whole point of the epithet was the clear understanding that there is no intrinsic incompatibility between consolation and thunder. There is no inconsistency between Christ's tenderness with children and harlots and His toughness with the self-righteous. The parable of the mustard seed and the reference to casting fire on the earth are not in necessary conflict. Love and violence are both parts of the gospel.

It is part of the irony of history that many contemporary Christians are shocked by any reference to the violent mood of early Quakers. Partly because of the Quaker emphasis on peace, the picture which has grown up in the modern world is that of a Quaker who is so tender and harmless and quiet that he is faintly ridiculous. Thus we have a current cartoon in which one little Quaker boy, looking unbelievably smug, says to another, "My father is gentler than thine." The development is ironic because the young men who emerged from the north of England in 1652, to go, with great boldness, to strange places where they they were destined to encounter harsh persecution, would not have got the point of the cartoon which makes us laugh so heartily. What this illustrates is the way in which the entire character of a Christian movement can change. The new beginnings are nearly always violent, but they tend to lose this character, particularly if they succeed.

What we need to understand, in our generation, is that Christianity is a much bigger thing than we are wont to suppose. We are engaged in a big enterprise—the enterprise of changing the whole world. The real heresy is not some failure in some detail of theological belief, but that by which we trivialize the Christian undertaking. It is real tragedy to make it little when it ought to be big. It is a terrible sin to make people think the gospel is equivalent to the elimination of some minor vice or anything negative. A Christian, in Christ's sense, is not marked by the little habits which he has or does not have, but by his willingness to share in a radical undertaking of a change in men's hearts and a consequent change in human history. Our baptism is total or none.

Herein lies our hope in the Christian cause today. Of course, we want to do all that we can for young people, and all who work with youth can speak with tenderness on this theme, but, in spite of our interest, honesty compels us to admit that the chance of a violent commitment to Christ on the part of the young is not very great now and will not be. That does not mean that our work with the young is unimportant. It is very important. It is important to sow the seeds, to develop the ground, to pray and to hope for the harvest, but the truth is that the harvest usually comes later. The harvest comes more often in maturity than before. It usually comes when people have lived enough to be hurt and to be disappointed and to face some tragedy and to recognize their own inability to manage.

God is always trying to reach our lives, but we put up barriers. We produce our own shells. God does not reach us until there is a crack in the armor, and the crack usually comes first in the form of a genuine crisis, when we are forced to realize that we are not self-sufficient masters of our own fate. This is exactly what happened to the lawyer. There was no chance for him so long as he thought he could manage, but there was a magnificent chance for God with him when he knew that he was inadequate. It is undoubtedly true that the greatest present opportunity for the growth of the Kingdom is to reach men and women of the character of this man.

As workers in the Cause of Christ we must become aware of a recognizable and much-repeated pattern in the lives we are trying to reach. The usual pattern, in modern America, involves youth in a mildly Christian home, with some years in Sunday School. A little of the gospel is thus learned at church, though not much is ordinarily learned at home. Often the father and mother, though they may give lip service to Christianity, are too self-conscious to pray in each other's presence or in the presence of their children. The children go to school or college, where they may have some vivid religious connections, but connections which are lost as they settle down to start their families and businesses or professions. These undertakings, along with social life and recreation, often take up almost the entire attention for several years. Life seems good; it is progressing; and there is abundant confidence in the ability to manage.

Sometimes this pattern of sufficiency goes on for nearly the whole of a person's career, but often there comes a break, which drives one either to despair or to new commitment. This break comes when a person, now fully adult, recognizes the superficiality of his own self-sufficiency and the need for some kind of new start. The crisis is not necessarily productive, but it may be, and in any case it represents a glorious opportunity. Frequently a man who has never been really touched by the gospel at all and has looked upon it as a pious gloss on a secular morality, finds, in a short time, a wholly new center of reference. A great many of the people who are most effective in the Christian movement today have come into it in this way. The very fact that the interest is fresh seems to be one reason for its tremendous appeal and the consequent revolutionary change. The fact that it can happen in middle life means that we dare never despair of any. We pray for the crisis and for God's redemptive use of it.

The practical conclusion for us to reach is the recognition that there must be a good many of us who are already vulnerable. There may be a much bigger life coming to us than we know; there may be greater steps ahead of us than we have ever dreamed. The life of full commitment is a life of such wonder that we ought to pray that God may bring us into it. But we cannot end with ourselves. Insofar as new life has come to us, we must try to bring new life to others. God, we are assured, desires new life for all, but it comes through human effort. Most people are reached one by one, as each is made to see both the inadequacy of his own life and the glory that might come in his life if he were really to give himself fully to the cause of Jesus Christ. But we must never suggest that such discipleship is easy or mild. Everyone who enters, says Jesus, enters violently or not at all. There is no easy Christianity; there is no mild Christianity. It is violent or it is nothing.

THE TRANSCENDENCE OF PRUDENCE

The master commended the dishonest steward for his prudence. LUKE 16:8

There are few passages of the Bible which are more puzzling than the story of the dishonest steward. If anyone is not puzzled by it, there is good reason to conclude that he has not really read it. The elements of the story are easy to comprehend; what is difficult is the total meaning of the parable and its bearing upon the gospel. On the surface it seems to be diametrically opposed to the bulk of Christ's teaching.

The story is of an employee who, having been reported to be cheating and wasting the goods of his employer, was summarily fired. That the report of his misdeeds must have been accurate is substantiated by the manner in which the man faced his loss of employment. He decided to use the last days, before the final severance from his job, to feather his own nest at his employer's expense. A great part of the parable is the following soliloquy:

What shall I do, since my master is taking the stewardship away from me? I am not strong enough to dig, and I am ashamed to beg. I have decided what to do, so that people may receive me into their houses when I am put out of the stewardship. So summoning his master's debtors one by one, he said to the first, "How much do you owe my master?" He said, "A hundred measures of oil." And he said to him, "Take your bill and sit down quickly and write fifty." Then he said to another, "And how much do you owe?" He said, "A hundred measures of wheat." He said to him, "Take your bill and write eighty."

Anyone can see that this is plain and obvious cheating. The man's only concern is for his own future welfare. He wants friends who are personally indebted to him and he achieves his end at the expense of another. He knows how to get what he wants and he is able to get it with no personal sacrifice. He is using people as instruments for his own ends. He uses both his employer and his employer's customers. Having been dismissed because of cheating, he is wholly consistent in that he continues to cheat as long as he can.

In view of this, wouldn't you suppose that the man would be condemned? Isn't that what you would think would be the conclusion of the story? But here is the shocking part that has puzzled all the more thoughtful people who have read it. "The master commended the dishonest steward for his prudence; for the sons of this world are wiser in their own generation than the sons of light. And I tell you, make friends for yourselves by means of unrighteous mammon, so that when it fails they may receive you into the eternal habitations." The man is dishonest; he is commended; and then Jesus tells us to go out and do the same kind of thing in order to make friends of the mammon of unrighteousness. Does that sound like Jesus? First, the man does an indecent act, but for this he is not criticized; he is commended. Second, Christ advises the disciples to do the same. To harmonize this with the rest of the gospel appears to be an impossible feat.

Our tendency, in dealing with the parable, is to avoid it as much as possible. Thus a brilliant Biblical scholar, in one of our best colleges, writes, "In a recent course on the parables I sidestepped this one." J. B. Phillips, to whom we

91

owe so much for his brilliant interpretations of all parts of the New Testament, elected to discuss this parable in a separate appendix when he undertook to paraphrase the Gospels and concluded by admitting the baffling character of the parable. Even Professor Torrey's suggestion of putting the offending sentences into question form does not satisfy him. If we, therefore, find this passage difficult, we are in good company. There is, of course, the possibility of denying the parable a place in the gospel record, but there is no valid reason for doing so. Since, textually, it is on as firm ground as anything else, our only reason for omission would be that it makes us uncomfortable. We dare not dismiss it merely because we do not like it. We must, therefore, try the better and the harder way of seeking a deeper meaning than that which appears on the surface.

A good place to start is with the commendation. Note that it is not Christ who commends the racketeer, but the employer. And for what does the employer commend him? Certainly not for his honesty, for that would have been impossible. He was *not* honest. The man in the parable was commended for only one thing—his prudence. And the truth is that he *was* prudent. Undoubtedly the employer was a prudent man, too, and knew he had met his match. In the art of looking out for number one the steward was extremely clever. If we leave out all ethical considerations, his action is, indeed, something to admire. If cleverness is the main thing, the man was superior. This is not surprising, for it is far easier to be clever if one is not handicapped by any concern for others. Those who are manipulating events, without any reference to moral values and responsibilities, have a freedom of action which conscientious persons can never enjoy. Having freedom from morality, they can move quickly in any direction which gives promise of being expedient. In this practical sense the children of this world are wiser, at least in their own generation, or temporarily, than the children of light can ever be. Leaders of a totalitarian regime have a freedom, and consequently an appearance of brilliance, which leaders of a responsible society can never hope to achieve.

When the story stresses the dishonest man's prudence it is simply telling the truth. He *was* prudent. The only reason why this disturbs us is that we have come to think of prudence as a Christian virtue. Our difficulty arises, then, not from the story itself, but from an unstated premise of our own making. Is there any reason to assume that all Biblical parables should be about good people? Who said that prudence is a Christian virtue? Not Jesus. We are helped by Christ's words to the effect that the best things are hidden from the wise and *prudent*. As so often occurs, then, we begin to find the solution of our problem by bringing out into the open a presupposition which loses its persuasiveness when it is openly examined. Though we have assumed prudence to be a Christian virtue, because it is a worldly virtue, this may be a point at which we are wrong. That it is a point at which we are wrong may be the chief teaching of the parable. The fact that the parable is difficult for us to accept is one of the reasons why it was necessary for Christ to tell it.

Though such a consideration helps mightily in the effort to understand the main part of the story, the conclusion is still difficult. Here Christ, speaking to the disciples, makes the application as follows: "And I tell you, make friends for yourselves by means of unrighteous mammon, so that when it fails they may receive you into eternal habitation." What can He possibly mean? He seems to be telling His followers to emulate the example of the steward in the story. He advises them to engage in a little corruption as a means of feathering their nests for the future. But here the future, preposterously enough, is not that of later success in life on earth, for which the dishonest steward prepared, but eternal life. The shocking fact is that Christ tells the disciples to engage in crooked and worldly deals in order to insure entrance into heaven. It is hard to see how anyone can read Luke 16:9 and not be profoundly disturbed by this text. We are disturbed because the contradiction with other New Testament teachings is absolute. Contrast, for instance, this commendation of friendliness to "unrighteous mammon" with words like these from an earlier chapter of the same gospel: "Sell your possessions, and give alms; provide yourselves with purses that do not grow old, with a treasure in the heavens that does not fail, where no thief approaches and no moth destroys. For where your treasure is, there will your heart be also" (Luke 12:33, 34).

Though the contradiction between Christ's advice about mammon and other parts of the gospel is sharp, we do not need to go to other parts, for the passage which follows immediately is a complete denial of what is said in Luke 16:9. Here is the passage:

He who is faithful in a very little is faithful also in much; and he who is dishonest in a very little is dishonest also in much. If then you have not been faithful in the unrighteous mammon, who will entreat to you the true riches? And if you have not been faithful in that which is another's, who will give you that which is your own? No servant can serve two masters; for either he will hate the one and love the other, or he will be devoted to the one and despise the other. You cannot serve God and mammon. [Luke 16:10-13]

In straight sober logic there is no way in which the mutual consistency of the two passages can be maintained. It cannot

94

be both good and evil to be cleverly unscrupulous. We have to choose. What then is the solution of the problem presented by the juxtaposition of inconsistent teachings? We can, of course, conclude that everything after the eighth verse is a later expansion, but that would be a mere speculation and entirely too easy a way out of the difficulty. We should need some kind of supporting evidence. Moreover, this leaves the original story so slight as to be hardly worth telling. The hypothesis which remains is that, in the parable itself, Jesus is joking. This hypothesis strikes us oddly at first, but this is only because we have sold ourselves on the untenable proposition that the Bible is always deadly serious. Why should it be? The more we examine the teachings of Christ the more we find hints of humor at a variety of points. Children, before they have been indoctrinated about the sobriety of the Bible, sometimes break into laughter when they first hear certain passages.

So long as we think Jesus was always serious, there is no reasonable way of making sense out of the advice to make friends with unrighteous mammon, but, if we recognize satire, the whole matter is clear. Probably the disciples laughed as they listened. In a modern paraphrase His satirical passage would be easily understandable. "You want to get ahead, do you? Then do it thoroughly. If you make bribes, make some big ones and cover your tracks. Always use cash and never a check. If you are put into prison make sure it is for a sheep rather than for a lamb. Remember to cultivate the right people, the people who have influence. If possible, get them in your debt, at least a little. If you are going to steal, don't steal from a bank. Steal the bank itself and then you may receive a doctor's degree!" However modern this seems, it is as old as human history and it is precisely what

Christ's sharp satire implies. Perhaps he found that it took satire to make the disciples see the point.

In the end the distasteful and satirical story becomes only a prelude to one of the grandest teachings of Christ which we encounter anywhere. This is one of the reasons for recognizing that the story of the dishonest steward is a significant as well as a difficult part of the gospel. The teaching which comes at the end, after the ironical mood is suddenly dismissed, is to the effect that the gospel is a greater break with the world than we ordinarily suppose. It is more radical than we at first realize. Christianity is not worldly prudence, with some religious words added. It is not the worldly wisdom of "God-fearing, money-making people." It does not put a premium upon sharp practice and canny dealing in which we learn, by the tricks of psychology, to use other men to our own advantage. It is, instead, a totally different kind of life.

One of the saddest things about the church, as we know it today, is that it is so much like the world. The great Christian boards are often run in almost the exact pattern of big business, and, even in the ministry, all of the tricks of getting ahead are both known and practiced on a wide scale. One good way to get an honorary degree is to enlist the help of a wealthy parishioner who, after making a donation to the church college, writes to say how suitable it would be for his pastor to be honored. The very emphasis on degrees and titles is quite as evident in church circles as it is in purely secular circles, in spite of the fact that Christ specifically warned not to be called "Rabbi." Church management is conducted as a worldly art, with direct mail advertising and many of the auxiliary enterprises of a successful business. We tend to make friends with mammon, and we do it with marked ability. There is no branch of the Christian Church which, in these matters, can afford to point the finger of scorn at others, without self-condemnation at the same time.

The real heresy is not the heresy of unbelief. The Bible has very little to say about unbelief. The real heresy is the watering down of the demands, making our Christianity the same as the pagan life around us, so that, after a while, it is just prudence and self-seeking, with a little veneer on top. This is not good enough. Such a weak faith will not win the world. It will not make the requisite difference in our civilization.

The Apostles found it difficult to understand the degree to which the gospel is a contrast to the world and, after all the intervening centuries of acceptance of Christianity, we find it even more difficult. Though most of the Apostles did not seek riches, they sought glory and this, Christ intimated, was a really serious barrier to faith. "How can you believe," He asked in John 5:44, "who receive glory from one another?" At no point is the break of original Christianity with worldly conceptions more clear than in regard to honor and at no point have we departed more thoroughly from the original pattern. The clearest statement of the radical nature of the Christian revolution is found in the following words of Christ: "The kings of the Gentiles exercise lordship over them; and those in authority over them are called benefactors. But not so with you; rather let the greatest among you become as the youngest, and the leader as one who serves" (Luke 22:25, 26).

Though it is not very surprising that men should fail to live up to the high demands of the gospel, it is both surprising and indefensible to fail to know what the character of these demands is. So long as we are able to read, we can see for ourselves that what Christ is calling us to join is a movement in sharp contrast to worldly standards. The discipleship to which we are called is far more exciting and far more costly than anything which the world normally knows. We are making at least a beginning at understanding what this means when we let Christ teach us that, for a Christian, prudence is not a virtue.

THE NECESSITY OF WITNESS

Let your light so shine before men, that they may see your good works and give glory to your Father who is in heaven. MATTHEW 5:16

Seldom is the gospel what we should like it to be. In no respect is this more clear than in Christ's insistence upon the necessity of public witness, for witness is one of the last acts in which we hope to engage. We want to be religious, of course, and not be blatant atheists like the Communist leaders, but we hope to practice our religion in some decently quiet and unostentatious manner. We really hope that it will not be necessary to talk about our faith at all. If possible, we avoid discussion of it in ordinary conversation, feeling far more secure if we can keep the conversation on a trivial level. The ideal is to avoid any suggestion of trying to influence others and this, we soon learn, can be done perfectly by keeping our faith as a personal and wholly private matter. This is why "I have my own religion" is such a familiar cliché. There are some things which cultivated people do not discuss and personal faith is one of them.

This conventional position of personal religious privacy is so common and so well accepted that we tend to forget that it is diametrically opposed to the teachings of Christ. It is really shocking for a modern man to read the Sermon on the Mount carefully, and to find that the very first commandment which Christ gave to the committed group on the mountainside was the command to share in public witness.

99

After telling the members of the group that it was their improbable vocation to be the salt of the earth, Christ's first requirement was that they should let their light shine.

We do not know whether this was hard for the original Apostles, but we do know that it is terribly hard for us today. We wish, devoutly, that He had said something else. It would have been so much easier if He had said, "Give a fair proportion of your income," or "Share in a work camp," or "Join a committee," or "Solicit for the community chest." To make a witness is one of the last things we are willing to do, because this seems to conflict with our unargued code of reticence. We are normally afraid of ostentation—that is, ostentation in our religious experience. We engage daily in ostentation in the cars we drive and the houses we own and the cities we build, but that, apparently, is another matter. In regard to faith, what we want above almost everything else is to avoid seeming pious. And the trouble about witness is that it seems like a public declaration of piety. Many, if they are sincere, will admit to a deep misgiving that, in this particular, Christ made a mistake. At least, they think, He made a mistake so far as our situation is concerned.

It is curious to see how we are more afraid of being sanctimonious than of being wicked. Many would hate worse to be called a saint than to be called a sinner. We never boast of our virtue, but we are extremely prone to boast of our vice. Some of those, particularly students, who were questioned in connection with the preparation of the Kinsey Reports on contemporary sex life, came out of the interviews telling how they had boasted of sins which they had never committed. In many circles this is the only way in which young people can save face at all. But, of course, this is far from new. In his *Confessions* written more than fifteen hundred years ago, Augustine of Hippo told with keen psychological insight how he had been "ashamed to be shameless."

100

We live in a period in which it is popular to be church members and even popular to attend public worship, but great numbers who attend are careful to attend in such a way that the personal involvement is kept at a minimum. That is why so many go to great lengths to try to occupy the back seats in places of public worship. By this means they—often unconsciously—become observers rather than participators. They maintain the "balcony view," seeking to be part of the audience rather than part of the cast and hoping to see rather than to be seen. "I'll come," is a common answer, "if I can slip in and out without having to do anything."

Within the last few years, during which there has been a remarkable growth in the practice of using lay readers for the presentation of the Scripture Lessons in churches of various denominations, the reticence concerning witness has been one of the chief elements of the general picture. Though many men and women bravely accept the task of public reading, and prepare carefully for it, there are others who refuse, and nearly always the refusal has something to do with Christian witness. "If I were to read the lesson," a common reply goes, "my neighbors would think of me as more deeply involved in the Christian life than I care to be. They would expect more of me in a religious way than I want them to expect." Those who make this frank reply show a deep insight. It is true that the act of reading becomes an act of witness, affecting not only the expectations of others, but also the way in which the man himself looks at his own life. He becomes thereby an insider; he has had the courage to show where he stands; henceforth he has a real stake in the Christian cause and is no more a benevolent outsider. But the very thing which the squeamish fear is what makes the practice of lay reading so valuable. Reading constitutes witness, and witness, when it is real, is twice blest. It blesses the one who witnesses and the one who listens.

We are clever enough to find ways of avoiding Christ's important command, without any loss of self-respect. The chief way in which we do this is to emphasize deeds rather than words, thus hoping to sound humble and also to avoid the embarrassment of words. A common expression is, "I don't speak to others about Christ; I just let my life speak." The more such a position is analyzed, the more arrogant it appears to be. It represents, in fact, not humility, but the acme of self-righteousness. Whose life is so good that his mere example, alone, is a sufficient witness? It is precisely because our lives are not good enough that we must also have the courage to witness by word. If our doctrine is not better than our lives, our lives will soon become worse than they now are.

The more we think about it, the more we realize that the fear of religious ostentation is almost wholly a misplaced fear. Christ does not tell us to let our lights shine in order to glorify ourselves, but in order to glorify God. My task is not to talk about my virtue, which in any case is nonexistent, but about the love of Christ to which, unworthy as I am, I can announce my dedication in the hope that others may be influenced to do the same.

It is not *our* religion that we, as Christians, are required to share. It is *Christ's*. The moment we try to hold our faith in such a way that we keep it to ourselves, and make no effort to influence other people who might be liberated by it, we are showing that we have a complete misunderstanding of the situation. "Any man who has a religion," said Robert E. Speer, "is bound to do one of two things with it, change it or spread it. If it isn't true, he must give it up. If it is true, he must spread it." The present tendency to renounce the missionary movement, on the ground of tolerance of all faiths, is a sign not of advance, but of intellectual confusion. A tolerance which blurs distinctions is no more valuable in religion than it is in science or any other realm. Concern for our fellow men does not mean leaving them to their own unaided devices, when a modest but courageous witness on our part could make a difference in their lives. The chief reason for the necessity of witness is the simple fact that thoughtful men are bound to share what they truly prize. If the gospel is true, our responsibility is to help to make it prevail. There is no place in Christianity for mere well-wishers. The task of contemporary Christians is to get out of the balcony and onto the witness stand.

Even after we accept the necessity of witness we may, nevertheless, be puzzled about the practical problem of how an effective witness is to be made. Certainly we do not think it is wise or helpful to approach strangers on the street with the question, "Do you know Christ?" The question is a valid one, but that way of asking it is likely to do more harm than good. We must be sure not to kill the thing we love. If we are to avoid this result we shall have to use a great deal of imagination.

A good example of effective witness, and one which may help others to see what their own may be, is that made recently by a Christian man in New York, in connection with the problem of race. This man, standing in line to ask for a room at a large hotel, noted that the man directly in front of him was a Negro whose conversation with the room clerk he could not avoid hearing. The clerk turned the Negro man away with the assertion that there were no unoccupied rooms. Then the white man, in his turn, asked for a room, for which he had no reservation, and the clerk replied, "Yes, certainly, what price did you have in mind?"

What was the white man's responsibility at this point? He was tempted, of course, to do nothing about the dishonesty, to be grateful for a room, and to tend to his own business.

"Don't borrow trouble," he said to himself. "You have enough of your own already." But there was something about the necessity of witness that would not let him rest. Accordingly, he noted that the Negro man had not yet left the hotel lobby, so he called to him to come back. "Come back," he said, "the clerk made a mistake. There *is* a room, because there is a room for me!" Then, turning to the clerk, he asked, "What are you going to do about it? You know the law of this state. I mean to see that it is enforced."

The result was that the clerk reversed his action and both men were given rooms. But this would not have occurred if the man in question had refused to let his light shine. He ran the risk of seeming to be a do-gooder and that, as everyone knows, is a bad thing to be.

A still more courageous witness, in regard to race, was shown by the Reverend Wade Boggs, a Presbyterian pastor of Little Rock, Arkansas, who, on the Sunday after the terrible trouble at Little Rock broke out, preached from his pulpit a powerful sermon on the way in which the gospel of Christ is incompatible with all discrimination on the basis of color. He placed the issue, not on the level of politics, but upon the level of dynamic religion. By doing so the pastor ran the risk of unpopularity, of loss of position and even of physical violence. It would have been so much easier, that Sunday, to preach on some purely theological issue. But to do so, he thought, would have meant a refusal to let his light shine. He took the opportunity to make clear the stand of the Presbyterian Church in the United States and in this he was not alone. A local editor made his own witness by publishing the sermon in full on the editorial page of his paper. Thus the witness of one man led to the witness of another.

There are many ways in which witness may be made. Some

make it by wearing a pin, some by openly reading the Bible while they travel, some by guiding conversation, even with strangers, into something more substantial than superficial chitchat. Others oppose these methods, but the opposition is hard to maintain in view of the fact that many lives have been deeply changed thereby. If the wearing of a pin leads to a conversation, by means of which even one person is brought into the Kingdom, it is wholly justified. Many can testify that the wearing of the black and red star of the American Friends Service Committee has been, in numerous cases, an effective means of witness, particularly in Europe.

Though it involves a certain courage, the simple act of bowing one's head in grateful prayer at the beginning of a meal, in a public dining room, is often more influential than would be supposed. Sometimes the unapologetic reverence of one man may start a chain reaction in which many others are involved. On the whole, public prayer is the simplest way in which a really vital witness can be made by the average Christian. We may discover, rather accurately, the spiritual vitality of a local church by finding out how many of the members are willing to engage, unashamedly, in public prayer. A church in which the pastor is the only person who can be counted on for vocal prayer, is a church that is already spiritually dead.

There are not many points at which an unapologetic witness is more needed than in connection with foreign aid. In this, our curious and almost pathological fear of sounding pious causes us to lean over backward to avoid telling what the real motivation of the far-flung enterprise is. We disguise it by making the sole justification our national self-interest. Perhaps self-interest is a relevant factor, but that this is the only factor is simply not true. We ought to have the forth-rightness and the courage to announce to the suffering and to the underprivileged that we are offering them aid as a Christian nation. To say that we are a Christian nation is not to say that we are personally righteous, but it is to say that Christian convictions have, for more than three hundred years, been powerful elements in the development of our culture. No one can hope to understand our civilization without reference to its Biblical roots. Many of the original colonists came to these shores for religious reasons and the continuity has never been wholly broken. We have not perfectly obeyed the precepts, but they have been an enduring source of disturbance to our complacency.

It might even be better to turn over the aid to religious agencies, Protestant, Jewish, and Roman Catholic, for administration. It is practically certain that it would, in that event, be administered more economically and efficiently. The problem of matching the mighty and disciplined faith of Marxism will not be solved by the loose impulses of a secular humanitarianism. How wonderful it would be if we could get over our spiritual timidity and openly declare that we, the unworthy children of God, are gladly trying to obey the precept to feed the hungry people, wherever they are. If anyone wishes to ridicule this and call it piety, let him; that is his business, not ours. Only in some such way can we recover the true dignity of our position. We must say, openly, that we are interested in the peoples of the undeveloped countries, not primarily because they are pawns in the cold war, but because they are made in the image of God, even as we are. We must have the courage to admit that we are interested in Africa, not merely because it is a rich continent, but because God, in His eternal music, plays upon the black keys as lovingly as He plays upon the white.

There is amazing power in the life of an individual or a church or a people, in which there is a willingness to make a witness, regardless of what people say. So long as we have our ears open for the remarks of others, much of our strength is dissipated. The way of power is that according to which we have our eyes on the task rather than on what people may think or say. If we are trying to be popular, we shall often be miserable, for human responses are notoriously fickle. The Christian answer is, "They say, let them say!" Our responsibility is not to win approval, but to be faithful. A faith about which we are apologetic is practically worthless. Herein lies the wonderful and enduring appeal of Paul's great witness in the first chapter of Romans, "For I am not ashamed of the gospel: it is the power of God for salvation to every one who has faith." On more than one occasion, a pastor, coming to the end of years of service in one place, has chosen these words for the text of the final sermon. It is not difficult to understand such a choice.

THE PROBLEM OF THE CROWD

When Jesus saw great crowds around him, he gave orders to go over to the other side.   MATTHEW 8:18

One of the advantages to be gained from reading the gospels in the Revised Standard Version is that the reader is likely, by the use of a fresh vocabulary, to see some parts of the familiar story in a fresh light. Such a light comes as we notice the frequent appearance of the word "crowd." Crowd is so much more striking than multitude. What we soon notice is not merely that there are many references to crowds in the pages of the gospels, but that these references appear very early. The public ministry of Christ was hardly started when the people began to press around Him in such a way as to make His work difficult.

In the rapid sequence of events in Mark's account we have the wilderness experience, the first preaching in Galilee, the call of Andrew, Simon, James, and John, the first teaching and healing at Capernaum and then, suddenly, great fame. "And at once," the account reads, "his fame spread everywhere throughout all the surrounding region of Galilee" (Mark 1:28). Soon, so many pressed about Him that He found it wise to retire to a lonely place for prayer "a great while before day." The disciples found Him in His retreat to announce that everyone was searching for Him, but this announcement, instead of drawing Him back to the waiting crowd, led directly to the decision to go to other towns. Very early Christ attracted crowds and very early He sought to escape them.

In Matthew's account, where the sequence is similar, we read, before the story of the Sermon on the Mount, that "his fame spread throughout all Syria" and "great crowds followed him from Galilee and Decapolis and Jerusalem and Judea and from beyond the Jordan." But here, also, Christ's response was escape from the popular following. "Seeing the crowds, he went up on the mountain" (Matt. 5:1). Some of the messages now grouped in Matthew 5, 6, and 7 must have been given to a large company, however, just as some were given to the few, for we read that "when Jesus finished these sayings, the crowds were astonished at His teaching" (Matt. 7:28). Again He found it expedient to escape, for, as the words of our text say, "Now when Jesus saw great crowds around Him, He gave orders to go over to the other side." If we understand this sentence we have a key to the understanding of much that Jesus was trying to accomplish.

That it was easy for Him to hold the attention of the people in large numbers is obvious. They loved to hear Him and they were attracted by His healing powers. It is clear that He could have gone on, from success to success, if He had been satisfied with this kind of a public career. The numbers, for a while, grew even larger. We are told that there were five thousand men, besides women and children, who came to Him in the desert. The populace pressed upon Him so closely by the sea that He had to go out to a boat in order to address them. There is no good reason to suppose that this popularity would have waned if Christ had been willing to encourage it. As a public speaker and as a healer He was undoubtedly a success. But a great deal of the gospel turns on the fact that this kind of success did not seem to Him to be sufficient.

One of the sad features of the gospel story appears in the recognition that the popular success, stunning as it was, was ephemeral. The crowds came and went and often there was no lasting effect at all. How sobering to realize that, at the end, when the going was hard and there was no miraculous feeding, the friendly crowds were almost entirely gone. Where were the five thousand when the crucifixion occurred? It was the crowd that chose the release of Barabbas instead of the brilliant speaker whom they had heard so gladly. Almost the only courageous ones at the bitter end were some women whose lives had been deeply changed by their contact with Christ.

The falling away of the crowds may surprise us, but it did not surprise Christ. Indeed, He predicted widespread defection. "And then many will fall away, and betray one another and hate one another. . . . And because wickedness is multiplied, most men's love will grow cold" (Matt. 24:10, 12). The Kingdom may come slowly, one by one, He suggests, but when defection sets in, it comes as a stampede. Jesus refused to depend upon crowds for the obvious reason that He knew them to be undependable. There is nothing in all this to suggest any snobbishness or any failure to appreciate the importance of each single individual among the five thousand. Instead, the meaning is the simple one that mere mass movements do not usually make any permanent impression. The permanent impression, if it comes, has to come in some other way. Christ's reason for turning away from the crowds was not any lack of love for persons, but an intense concern for a cause. We have good evidence that Christ loved the people in the crowds and had deep sympathy for them. This is suggested by the sentence, "When he saw the crowds, he had compassion for them, because they were harassed and helpless, like sheep without a shepherd." He was so touched by their pain and confusion that it must have been difficult to turn from them, again and again, in order to pray alone or to instruct the inner group.

Christ must have considered deeply the problem of how the gospel could possibly succeed. Expecting, as He did, His tragic death, the great problem was that of continuance after the end of His earthly appearance. It is easy to see that a great mob of undisciplined, wonder-seeking people would have no power of endurance at all. They could be scattered in an hour. The only hope, then, lay in the formation, while there was time, of a veritable Gideon's band. Could He find a few willing men and train them with sufficient intensity to make sure that they could carry on? Here was the only hope and even this was risky, as defections within the inner group later showed. These had to be formed into a tough, commandolike company, carefully indoctrinated in the principles which the crowd could not understand, warned of impending danger and loved into newness of life. Not very good stuff was available for this task force, but He used the best that there was. This He did by calling them, one by one. First He recruited and then He trained. It must have been the dire necessity of giving this task force all of the attention which time permitted that limited Christ's attention to the crowd. He could not attend to both at the same time.

The need of building up a committed inner circle explains features of the gospel which otherwise are not understandable. One of the chief of these is the way in which, in marked contrast to our ordinary contemporary procedure, Jesus warned His would-be followers against easy joining. This surprises us because we practically beg people to join and we are a little shocked when we realize that, so far as we know, Christ did not beg anybody.

111

After Christ had deliberately left crowds on one side of the Sea of Galilee to go over to the other side away from them, individuals came to Him as potential recruits. One said, with manifest enthusiasm, "Teacher, I will follow you wherever you go." We should expect an equally enthusiastic response of acceptance, but Christ did not give it. Instead He deliberately tested the man, by making him realize the serious dangers which such recruitment might involve. The only reply was the warning that discipleship might mean privation. "Foxes," He said, "have holes and birds of the air have nests; but the Son of Man has nowhere to lay his head." Immediately after this, another potential volunteer was found unsatisfactory because he made an excuse for postponement on the ground of private responsibilities. Only those could be accepted on the task force who would give it absolute priority. It was bigger business than the superficial enthusiasts supposed. However important family ties were, the demands of the gospel took precedence over them and, in some cases, might even cause divisions.

It is really hard to understand how Christ got any recruits at all, in view of the stern picture of their life which He presented. He told them they would be sent out as sheep in the midst of wolves, that they would be flogged and beaten and delivered up to death. The disciples could not reasonably expect a life any easier than that of their Master. Herein lies the poignant appeal of the question, "Are you able to drink the cup that I am to drink?" The hard demands undoubtedly had the effect which they have on any potential Gideon's Band; they kept the group small. Consider, for example, the reducing effect of words like these: "If any man would come after me, let him deny himself and take up his cross daily and follow me."

The would-be followers may not have known all that was

meant by the cross, but they certainly knew that it meant something tragic. The cross had something of the significance, in the ancient world, that the gallows and the gas chamber have in ours. It was not a piece of jewelry to be proudly worn. In fact, nearly all of the major symbols used by Christ were offensive, from the point of view of ordinary worldly standards. The cup was the cup of sorrow, the yoke was the instrument of toil, the towel was the symbol of the status of a servant, the sword was that which pierced. The wonder is that there were any Apostles at all! Nearly the whole of Christ's strategy is explained in one short passage in Luke.

Now great multitudes accompanied him; and he turned and said to them, "If any one comes to me and does not hate his own father and mother and wife and children and brothers and sisters, yes, and even his own life, he cannot be my disciple. Whoever does not bear his own cross and come after me, cannot be my disciple. For which of you, desiring to build a tower, does not first sit down and count the cost, whether he has enough to complete it." [Luke 14:25-28]

Here is the essence of the warning in three short words, "Count the cost." Christ wants followers, but He does not want them to start unless they have a full understanding of the perils of the road that stretches out before them. To start and not to be able to finish is worse than not to start. "No one who puts his hand to the plow and looks back is fit for the kingdom of God." Here, then, is an enterprise into which only the bold and the hardy are encouraged to enter. Though we do not usually realize it, the twelve men finally selected must have been only a fraction of those who applied. Perhaps there were hundreds who heeded the warning and went their way, convinced that they could not drink the cup that Christ drank. In the words of John 6:66, they "drew back and no longer went about with him."

113

What a great event the selecting of the Twelve was! Much of the future history of the world hinged on the decision about these men. If all should prove to be unfaithful, as Judas did, what then would happen to the plan for saving mankind from ultimate decay? According to Luke's account, Christ took the decision about the appointment of the Twelve so seriously that he spent all of the previous night alone in the hills, in prayer. This is not really surprising, when we realize how momentous the occasion was. He was already withdrawing from the crowds, and now it was these or nobody. From then on the great majority of his reported effort was expended upon the careful preparation of these men for their subsequent testing. What was needed was a society hard enough to penetrate thick barriers, something which an amorphous mass can never do.

There is a strange irony in the fashion in which the modern Communist movement has taken over some of the features of Christianity, directing some of the same strategy to other and different ends. One of the really critical moments came in London, more than fifty years ago, when, at an international Communist meeting, Lenin barely won out in his struggle to limit the membership of their group to a small, disciplined and deeply committed body of men. If Lenin had not won at that point, the subsequent history of mankind would undoubtedly have been very different. To this day the victories of militant communism are won, in every case, not by a majority, but by a highly disciplined, unyielding, and dedicated minority. Always it is the prepared task force which takes over.

The more we meditate upon Christ's method, the more we realize that the Twelve and those closely associated with them had many of the characteristics of an underground movement. Only on the basis of this understanding can we

114

explain the frequent injunctions concerning secrecy. Even the account of the preparations for the final meal with the Twelve sounds like a contemporary story of a secret meeting of a rebel group under the very eyes of the police. There was, above all, a prearranged signal concerning the place of meeting. "Behold, when you have entered the city, a man carrying a jar of water will meet you; follow him into the house which he enters, and tell the householder, 'The Teacher says to you, Where is the guest room?'" This is precisely the kind of procedure we expect in the meeting of a secret society. How else, except on the basis of a good deal of secrecy, can we explain the necessity of paying a large bribe to Judas to act as an informer? If all of the operations of the little company were as open as Christ's visits to the temple area were, no canny group of leaders would have paid any money at all, for they could have found the group themselves. We are drawn to the conclusion that, while some of the operations of the Twelve were public, others were not. In any case all of the members of the group were highly aware that they were engaged in an enterprise as risky as it was important.

The lesson of all this for our day and generation is the lesson that there are times when we too must withdraw from the crowds. We can be glad that we live in a period in which church attendance is more common than it has been for a long time, and in which mass evangelism has been renewed, but we ought to be aware that there is no spiritual security in this kind of success. It is easy to get crowds and it is likewise easy to lose them. There are predictable circumstances in which we *shall* lose them.

Perhaps the church, in many areas, must be smaller before it can be substantially stronger. The words and the actions of Jesus must always remind us that hope lies, not primarily in numbers, but far more in the quality of commitment. It is because Christ has compassion on the crowds that He leads us today to build up new task forces by means of which the life of the multitude may be made less confused. The love of the masses leads to emphasis on the few.

It is strange that Christians, with the example of the gospel in mind, would be so easily deluded by the fallacy of bigness. Yet it is sadly true that the success of a modern church is often judged by the number of members, and the success of a pastor is sometimes measured by the number of accessions. We can always be happy about accessions, providing the growth is real, but we know very well that often it is not real at all. Sometimes there is no period of probation, no training or preparation, no real evidence of a changed life. Sometimes there is nothing but the one question, "Do you accept Jesus Christ as your Savior?", a question which is naturally answered in the affirmative, and then one more is counted in the struggle for statistical victory. The trouble with this procedure is that verbal "acceptance of Christ" may mean much or it may mean almost nothing. Jesus Himself understood this so well that He dealt with it specifically by saying, "Not every one who says to me, 'Lord, Lord,' shall enter the kingdom of heaven" (Matt. 7:21).

Just as there is no spiritual security in the presence of a crowd, so, on the other hand, there is none in smallness. Some movements are small, not because of any excellence, but simply because they are dull and lifeless. Some, who make disparaging remarks about the ability of others to draw large numbers, are merely jealous, and would have them if only they could. The Christian movement goes forward, not because of bigness and not because of smallness, but by the reality of the new life which is demonstrated.

116

We may say truly of crowds what is said of ceremonies in Galatians 6:15, "For neither circumcision counts for anything, nor uncircumcision, but a new creation." Neither the presence of crowds nor the absence of crowds can give any occasion for complacency. What we seek is a new creation.

THE
EMERGING
ORDER

Behold, I have given you authority to tread upon serpents and scorpions, and over all the power of the enemy; and nothing shall hurt you. LUKE 10:19

The Christian Movement of today needs a change of mood. Our fundamental handicap arises from the fact that the Christian faith has long been taken for granted in the Western world, and the consequences are many and disastrous. For millions our religion involves neither urgency nor excitement, for it is difficult to be urgent about the obvious and the secure. Our popular religion has become both lukewarm and well-mannered, neither feared, admired, nor hated by those outside it, and not fiercely defended by those on the inside. It is neither hot nor cold. Insofar as our conventional religion is failing, it is failing not because it is either radical or conservative in political conceptions, and not because it is modernist or fundamentalist in theology, but simply because it has lost the sense of urgency. As we envisage the entire strategy of the church at this point in history, we must find some way to recover the urgency or we are lost. The mood we seek to engender must somehow include the rank and file of members, rather than merely a chosen few who have some special reason to know what our predicament is. How can the new mood be produced? This is our central question, if we are interested in the practical undertaking.

In answering this question, as is the case with so many

118

others, we are wise to turn to the gospel story to learn again what Christ's own method was. At no point in the story is the mood of urgency more clear than in the account of the sending out of the Seventy. Partly because of this, those who are today committed to the lay apostolate are increasingly drawn to the tenth chapter of Luke. We turn repeatedly to this passage because it shows how Christ could infuse, in others than the Twelve, a sense of responsibility for the promotion of His work. We do not know who the individuals among the Seventy were, but we know the mood in which they were commissioned and we know of their remarkable success. They moved with a power that seems to have been surprising even to themselves. Christ sent them out as lambs among wolves; He told them to take no excess baggage; and He told them not to waste precious time. In short, they constitute what we should call a task force. They were asked, not to attend a meeting, but to participate in a difficult and dangerous encounter. They were as far removed from the status of observers as from that of professionals. In one sense they were of the rank and file, but, in another sense, they constituted a hard core.

As a result of much study of this passage we are beginning to have a clearer vision of what the contemporary counterpart of the Seventy may be. While there are still millions who think that joining a church is just another helpful connection in a neighborhood, there are minorities in all parts of the Christian movement who recognize that it is more like joining a campaign. In all denominations there are leaders who have caught this vision of membership as enlistment. They know that we have lost much ground; they are often frightened as they contemplate what the future may hold for their children; and in consequence, they are willing to begin by joining a movement devoted to the recovery of the lost provinces of the Christian faith. Deeply shaken by a new vision of the meaning of the Christian faith, they are willing to devote their lives to its promotion, wherever this devotion may lead them. The idea that is developing so powerfully is the idea of an order. An order is a society of persons, united by some common rule of obligation. The reformation that is sought is that by which the church as we know it becomes an order in this sense.

One of the most impressive developments of all history is that of the organization and guidance of the Society of Jesus by Ignatius Loyola. Loyola, in the sixteenth century, saw the Roman Catholic faith apparently losing at all points, as the Roman Empire had been losing a thousand years earlier. He determined to found an order dedicated to the reversal of the process. His dream was that of a militant order devoted to the recovery of the lost provinces of the faith he loved. The whole thing became exciting because it was a campaign. The losses were obvious, the dangers were real, the task was urgent. The Jesuit success was, and still is, phenomenal, the success apparently stemming largely from the way in which the whole undertaking has been envisaged.

We may take this historical development to heart and apply it to our current situation. There is no hope for the survival of the kind of Christianity we prize unless adherence to the church becomes adherence to a cause. The church must become a militant order for the recovery, the extension and the application of a glorious faith. If we can remake the church into an order devoted to the recovery of the lost provinces, there is enormous hope. We have a wonderful faith; we have a Risen Lord; what we need is a way of remaking the church according to Christ's pattern.

The order we seek must begin within the church as we know it, working constantly from within to alter the character of the church. Sometimes we can have only two or three willing to begin, but to start with that many is better than not to start at all. We must remember that what we seek is, in all situations, a reformation within the church and not a reformation from the church. To set up a new denomination would be easy, but it would be almost worthless at this point. What is needed, by contrast, is a movement of great power which cuts across all denominational lines, so that those who are working for the recovery of the lost provinces in the Methodist Church will feel a deep sense of unity with those who are doing the same in the Presbyterian Church, though this horizontal loyalty never interferes with the denominational loyalty. This is exactly what is coming to pass, and it presents no conflict of loyalty whatever. Because an order is radically different from a denomination, loyalty to both at the same time involves no difficulties. We must be wary of new religious movements which tend to draw people away from their local churches. What we seek, instead, is a movement which, by the inculcation of a new mood and the encouragement of a new discipline, can make ordinary Christians more effective members where they already belong and where their contributions are needed.

The Society of Jesus, as developed so imaginatively by Ignatius Loyola in the sixteenth century, had certain features which we should emulate today and certain features which we should reject. There are four features which we should reject, as follows: First, it was devoted to recovery in only one denomination; namely, the Roman Church. Certainly the brave men who answered Loyola's call, often going out into terrible danger at a time of mutual religious persecution, were not interested in helping the Reformed faith to prevail. Such narrowness brings a certain strength, but, in

121

the long run, it is a mistake. Every sincere Christian, no matter how loyal to his own denomination he may be, must try to remember Christ's own words, "Other sheep have I that are not of this fold." In contrast to the Jesuit order, we hope for an order which is devoted to the promotion of more than one branch of Christianity.

In the second place, we are bound to reject the principles of an order which is limited to one sex. There are, undoubtedly, occasions when it is good for men to work alone as men, and occasions when it is good for women to work alone as women, but the great task of inner reformation in the church is such that it needs both men and women all the time. There are real differences between the sexes, but, in the major work of Christ, there is neither male nor female. Men and women should keep the same disciplines and undertake the same kinds of advancement of Christ's cause.

A third difference is that, whereas Loyola's task force was limited to what we call the clergy, we cannot allow such a limitation in the new order that is emerging. Neither can we limit it to the laymen. There is a deep level of commitment in which clergy and laymen can be united and where they work better if they work, side by side as participants in a common cause.

A fourth point where we must differ from the sixteenth-century model is in regard to separation from common life. We do not seek an order in which there is such separation as is implied by a rule of celibacy or a rule of absolute poverty. The men and women who live a separated life undoubtedly have a certain freedom from ordinary responsibilities and thus approach their religious duties with a consequent singleness of attention, but they will always represent a special class in society. What we need is people in common life, with jobs and responsibilities and home and children and who, in spite of these, are nevertheless engaged in the development of the new order. Participation means more when it comes under such circumstances.

As we try to consider the features of earlier orders which we can emulate, we may mention first the acceptance of "holy obedience." One of the most wonderful features of the early Jesuit Order was the way in which a member was expected to pull up stakes and go, if necessary, to the ends of the earth. Everyone had to live loosely to life, ready to shift his sphere of operations if the cause to which he was devoted should demand it. Each had to be willing to have new chapters in his life, if new chapters should be required.

We see something of how this could operate among our new shock troops when we think of a man like the late Clarence Johnson, of St. Louis. This remarkable man suddenly gave up, at the age of fifty-seven, his influential position as a vice-president of the Purina Mills and started a wholly new chapter of his life, because he felt that loyalty to the gospel demanded it. The last eighteen months of his life were, he said near the end, the most wonderful of all, though they were far less secure. The time may come when, with a minority of Christians, such a pattern of decision and action may come to be entirely normal and in no sense the exception. Perhaps the time can come when, in addition to our great organized missionary work around the world, deeply committed men and women may give up security and do creative things for the Christian cause either at home or abroad. This would not be new in Christianity, though it might be new to us.

Early Christianity seems to have been exciting partly because the new members lived dangerously. God might lead them any day to pull up stakes and go far away to try to start a new chapter of the sacred Order. Whenever we have, in subsequent years, experienced primitive Christianity revived, this aspect of Christian experience has been one of the first to appear. For example, in the early Quaker Movement of three hundred years ago it was an unargued assumption that each Friend was, by definition, an evangelist. In the tiny Quaker group which met at Swarthmore Hall from 1652 to 1690, no less than twenty members went out as missionaries. They went to Holland, Germany, Barbados, New England, Turkey, and many other places near and far. This missionary activity was at once a symptom of their religious vitality and a cause of further vitality.

A second positive mark of the new order, which we can adopt from many successful ones in the past, is that each Christian, insofar as he is part of the development, will give his Christian obligation a certain priority over all others. Because the members of the new order are people engaged in common life, and never separated from it, they naturally have many responsibilities as citizens. Some should belong to luncheon clubs, some to parent-teacher organizations, some to labor unions, some to veterans organizations. Each of these is a field for the entrance of the gospel, if we represent it with humility and sincerity. But, while this is true, it is also true that the very multiplicity of organizations may come to dominate a Christian's life so completely that the Christian vitality is dissipated.

Recently an accurate survey revealed the discouraging news that, in a town of seventeen hundred persons, there are only five churches, but fifty-six clubs. Naturally the level of participation in the life and work of the churches is low, one reason for such poor participation being that so much of the energy of alleged Christians is drawn off in secular pursuits. After members have met the demands of the American Legion, the parent-teacher association, the labor union, the literary club, and the sorority, there is little time or imagination left for the promotion of the Christian cause. Unfortunately the church is looked upon by many as just another one of these fifty-six clubs, but with a certain difference in that its demands may be less strict. After all, a Rotarian is required to attend the weekly luncheons of his club on pain of dismissal, but the ordinary church is not so unkind.

What we must say about these many organizations is that most of them are basically good and serve good ends. Certainly they are not evil, and Christians ought to work in many of them in order to apply the Christian witness to the work of the ordinary world. But if we begin to look upon the Church as a society of Christian obligation, we soon realize that we must establish some kind of priority in the employment of time, money, and energy.

We shall not get very far until we establish, within each church, a hard core of men and women who have sufficient toughness to put the promotion of the Christian cause first in their lives. What if, let us say, we have a group who form the "New Seventy" and who go out once a week, two by two, somewhat as the original Seventy did, to try to reach new people as Christ's emissaries? And then what if, on the night regularly set aside for this task, there should come a benefit performance put on by some local society? Perhaps it is not possible to give an absolutely inflexible answer to this question, but the general answer is that, except for the most extreme cases, the problem should not be a problem at all. In any event, we shall not bring back the Christian vitality we need until we have groups who follow a discipline of time so clear that they give unhesitating priority for the Christian obligation. We have a few Christian organizations which work on this principle now and all of them make an impact on society out of all proportion to their size.

Thus we are beginning to have some vision of what the new militant Seventy could be in our day. The members are not greatly concerned about building up a new complex organization of their own, but are deeply concerned about bringing new life into the existing organizations to which they already belong. They do not wish to be divisive or separatist, but they do wish to strengthen one another, to inspire mutual imagination, and to learn from one another. They need to come together once in a while, not primarily for their own self-enjoyment, but chiefly in order to strengthen themselves for their task within the church, which is almost identical, regardless of their denominational affiliation.

To this end we need places in the modern world which are, to the task of modern conversion, what, in the Dark Ages, Iona was to the conversion of Scotland. In this as in so much else, we are foolish if we refuse to learn from the Communists in their remarkable success in the last half-century. Only the blind can fail to be impressed by the fact that the Communists have moved, in fifty years, from nearly nothing to the domination of the lives of more than eight hundred million persons. In all this the guiding force has been a hard core of the entirely committed. Central to their enterprise has been the Lenin Institute of Moscow. This we ought to understand as much as we are allowed to do. To this are sent the dedicated ones who, in their study, learn how to penetrate other societies and to take over when the time is ripe. It was to this that the present leaders of Communist China were sent years ago. They were learning the task of revolution and preparing for their present duties when most of us in the West were being complacent about China, never dreaming that the victory of those at the Institute would be so great so soon.

What we need is Christian counterparts of the Lenin Institute, strategically located. We may need to develop a new kind of education in these, widely different from what is now found in a standard theological seminary. The students will be of any denomination, they will include both men and women, they will include both clergy and laymen, and they will be people who expect to live out their religious vocations in common life. Some of these features are found in some educational institutions today, but what will be most different in the Christian counterparts of the Institute at Moscow will be the mood of dedication. All will be in preparing for membership in the Christian Army of Occupation, dreaming up new ways of penetrating secular society and reaching men's minds. Some will learn to write for newspapers, some to work in labor unions, some in universities, some to speak on street corners, and others to perform tasks which we do not now envisage at all, but which we shall envisage if we begin to join together in the effort to develop not only holy obedience, but a holy imagination.

Thus we see some of the marks of the new order that must emerge and that is already beginning to emerge, but we do not see nearly enough. We may be encouraged, however, by the words of our Lord when He said, "I have yet many things to say to you, but you cannot bear them now" (John 16:12). Our hope and our faith is that, as the new order of Christ develops, we may be able to bear the new things which Christ has to say to us and to our generation.

127

THE
DISCIPLINE
OF
DISCIPLESHIP

Train yourself in godliness.
I Timothy 4:7

The acceptance of the idea of discipline has come more rapidly and more widely than anyone supposed that it could. This has occurred through a combination of factors, one of which is the public recognition of the weaknesses of progressive education. Though there are still many of our people who resist discipline of any kind, and particularly self-discipline, the idea that excellence can be achieved without some system of control is no longer convincing to anybody. We cannot help but see that the men who have achieved wonders in modern science and technology are men of very great inner discipline. Not one has succeeded by following the path of least resistance.

There is a great deal of power in the world, including human power, but much of it is wasted because it is neither controlled nor directed. The stream which flows hither and yon over the lowlands, is not useful as a source of power, even though it may carry a large volume of water. On the other hand, quite a small stream, if it is guided into a mill race, with sharp banks which prevent waste, may turn a large wheel and provide useful energy for the tasks which men need to have done. What counts is not total volume, but the power that is directed.

Something of a similar nature occurs in regard to the power of men. Human energy is wasted if it is not harnessed. Herein lies the major significance of the third Beatitude, "Blessed are the meek for they shall inherit the earth." Ordinarily this affirmation is difficult for us to understand, because "meekness" seems to us such a weak virtue, but the meaning is greatly enhanced when we realize that the Greek word here translated "meek," is closely allied to the idea of being "harnessed" and therefore trained. What is suggested is the contrast between the harnessed animal and the wild animal. In spite of the attractiveness of the latter, it is the former which wins the wilderness. Empty freedom is never as effective as directed power.

We see the truth of this, vividly, in such well-known human achievements as athletics and music. The athlete who is training for a contest does not dare to relax his discipline for a single day. Thus Bob Richards, when he was at the height of his powers as a pole vaulter, crossed the nation by car and stopped at a different athletic field each day in order to keep in trim. The absolute regularity of the training was far from convenient, but it was the price of excellence. In the same fashion, the concert pianist takes his piano with him, even when he crosses the ocean by ship. The price is high and it is unrelenting. The fact that most people are unable to play the piano, with any skill, comes partly from lack of talent, but it comes also from lack of discipline. We are not *free* to place our fingers unerringly on the right keys, not because we do not know what the keys are, but because we have not paid the adequate price for that kind of freedom. Most of us have great energy, but we waste it most of the time.

What we have now rediscovered, with a good deal of understandable enthusiasm, is that the same principles, which apply to science and athletics and music, apply equally to our religious experience. Once it was modish to claim absolute freedom in such matters, looking with condescension on those who were bound by a rule, but such condescension is now out of date. We cannot help but see that those who have a rule to live by seem to have more power available. If, in a given city, there are more Roman Catholics than Protestants participating in public worship on a Sunday, there is just one major reason for the difference; the Roman Catholics are the more disciplined body. They are like soldiers at drill.

It was especially noticeable among the troops in the war that about the only ones who held on to a vital faith were those who maintained some kind of strict practice. This was often true, regardless of the particular features of that practice. Thus the orthodox Jews, distinguished from their fellow soldiers by the rigid Sabbath observance each Friday night, have something strong enough to hold them together. If it had been Thursday night it would have been equally effective. The point is that there was *something* which these men did and did with regularity, independent of their passing whims. A certain toughness was thereby built into their lives.

There was a time when liberal-minded people criticized this kind of discipline because of the fear of Pharisaism, but anyone can see that overstrictness is not our danger now. Our present danger is that of laxity, of laziness, of self-indulgence, of the rejection of all authority. The peril we face is seldom that of narrowness, but frequently that of becoming diffuse. We scatter our lives in every direction, doing too many things and doing none well. We have too many concerns, which is almost as bad as having none. We are like the river which flows all over the bottomland in many different beds and consequently never turns a turbine at all.

This is where the realization that the Christian faith demands narrow banks is such a beneficent discovery. We are beginning to see the wonderful truth that a Christian is one who is harnessed, wearing Christ's yoke and thereby renouncing empty freedom. We see new significance in the Christian teaching that, whereas the way which leads to destruction is broad, the way which leads to life is intrinsically narrow. The Christian, we now know, is not one who does as he pleases, but one, instead, who seeks to please his Lord.

One result of this discovery is an increased determination to say "No" to many appeals. Thus a man who moves over from mere secularism to a conscious discipleship is likely to reduce, rather than to enlarge, the number of his public interests. The growth is not one of scattering, but of concentration on a few. A man who examines his public life and finds that he has fifteen or twenty public responsibilities, ought to be tough enough with himself to reduce this number to four or five. It will require a severe self-discipline to keep life thus reduced, but it is a necessary price if discipleship is to be really effective.

The place for most of us to begin, therefore, is with the discipline of time. While we are alive, time for all men is equal, because each has twenty-four hours a day, but we are extremely unequal in the ways in which we use these precious hours. Some men accomplish ten times as much as others, not primarily because they have conspicuous talents, which others do not have, but more often because they use each day well. There are those who, in the horrible popular phrase, "kill" time; there are others who think they are accomplishing something when they are merely fretting; there are some who get down to business and *use* time, because they see each day as God's gift.

We should make it very clear that the waste of time is a

sin, and it is a sin because there are so many things that ought to be done, for the sake of human welfare. This is not to say that men ought always to labor. There is, indeed, a time to play, but play is good as a use of time because it is, or can be, creative, leading subsequently to the release of new powers. Much of the secret of the discipline of time lies in the decision to divide life into chapters, with some periods for work, some for family enjoyment, some for play, some for prayer, etc. Perhaps there ought to be some time devoted to complete idleness, but even so, this should be only a fraction of the total time.

The chief way in which a great many people fail in the discipline of time is in the postponement of sleep at the end of the day. The next morning is ruined, for the most part, the night before. To be strict with oneself about retiring is not easy, because the temptations to stay up are endless, but the results of strictness in this regard are wonderfully rewarding. Full energy in the most creative part of the day is something so good that one may reasonably pay a price for it. One of the greatest hindrances to public worship on Sunday morning arises from the ways in which Saturday nights are spent. People who have had only a few hours of sleep should not expect much of a sense of reality in the experience of worship. Perhaps the ancient Jews, in the institution of the Sabbath, were right to start it at sundown the night before.

The worship of Almighty God is an enterprise of such importance that no one should expect to find it easy. Why should it be easier to learn to worship God than to practice medicine or to develop any other human skill? We need, in this enterprise, to learn all that we can from one another, realizing that, even at the end, we shall be imperfect and inept. In spite of our amateurishness in these high matters, there are a few things about the discipline of worship that we know. One is that we must make it an inflexible rule to enter the worshiping group in total silence. There are times for pleasant conversation about trivial matters, but this is not one of them. Just as the pole vaulter disciplines his muscles, the worshiper must discipline himself to keep his voice still, his body still, and his mind still. The ancient rule still holds, "Be still and know."

At first it is hard to keep our thoughts from wandering fruitlessly from one worldy interest to another, but, by constant practice, the task becomes easier. It is especially helpful to fasten upon some great theme or some important human need until this object of attention opens the door at which the living Christ is always knocking. By stages we can train ourselves to follow a pattern which begins with adoration of God's love, which goes on to our own unworthiness and consequent sense of repentance, and ends with the dedication of our lives to such humble service as inadequate persons like ourselves can perform. This pattern of worship, which received its classic statement in Isaiah's account of his call, may be profitably compared to the pattern of discipline which has long been found relevant in learning scientific method. The main thing to remember is that there is no good reason to expect worship to be easy. All great things are hard.

The area of experience in which we have learned most about religious discipline is that which is known as private devotion. Here, a few points are reasonably clear. For one thing we know that our public religious life is likely to be thin and shallow if the inner disciplines, especially those relating to prayer and to scripture, are not kept up with absolute regularity. Prayer is obviously central. Nearly all private religion is private prayer and nearly all public religion is public prayer. One of the most fruitful of all disciplines is that by which the individual begins and ends the conscious experience of each day with prayer. The beginning may take the form of the "Plotted Day," a practice generally accepted in the Iona Community. What this means is that the person involved starts each day by going deliberately through the day in advance, asking God's help in each foreseeable circumstance. We cannot know all that any new day will include, but we can be reasonably certain of several responsibilities and decisions. It is in these that we most need God's help to supplement our own finite wisdom. The day may still include elements of novelty, but one valuable result of this practice of the Plotted Day is that events begin to sort themselves out in new ways. The big things become big and the small things become small. Nearly always some rearrangement of priorities is the practical outcome of prayer at this level.

Prayer at the end of the day is a natural conclusion, as the humble penitent commits the finished day to God's care and accepts thankfully the opportunity for rest, sure of the need for new strength on the morrow. The discipline of such set times for prayer does not preclude the experience of spontaneous prayer at all times in the day. It is good, of course, to pray unceasingly, but we are more likely to do so if we develop, with conscious intent, the habit of set times. Eventually these become as much second nature as is the practiced vaulter's stride as he carries the pole.

Our private prayers are likely to be far richer if we supplement them by the regular use of materials which come from outside ourselves. Many are helped by the steady use of classic prayers and by the study of the great books of devotion, but, for most people, nothing is more helpful than a daily encounter with the Bible. Here we need to be concrete and practical. Many wish to read the Bible, but they do not know how to begin. Often they try to read too much at a time, with the result that the total impact is superficial and the reader usually feels hurried.

Increasingly, we see that the ideal method of Bible reading is to peruse, prayerfully and carefully, a small section each day, never allowing an exception, unless there is some emergency such as illness. If this is done at the same time each day, perhaps just after breakfast, it comes to be a sort of hub of the day's experience and is remembered easily after a few weeks of unbroken practice. For a good while it is wise to go straight through several books in this way, in small daily sections, dating each section when it is completed. The dating avoids self-deception and the continuance through entire books avoids the scattering of interest that has so often marked Bible reading. By studying twelve or thirteen verses a day in this way, the devout reader can go carefully in one year through the Four Gospels and the book of Acts.

Many seem to have missed the great value that comes from reading the Bible with pen or pencil in hand. But the discipline of steady marking may be one of the chief values of the entire undertaking. It is good to underline, to question, and to comment. It is even better to use the blank pages sometimes found at the end, to express ideas which tend to grow by the very act of expression.

Many, who are otherwise devout, have missed the strength that comes from writing their own prayers. Probably it has not occurred to them to do so, but they might find the experience surprisingly valuable if they would try it. Of course our prayers, as written, may seem very poor in comparison to the great models, but there is no harm in that. The writing of personal prayers was one of the chief secrets of the robust spiritual life of the great Dr. Samuel Johnson. We can see the strong man's prayers in his own handwriting today, just as he left them, and when we look at them we can visualize his spiritual struggles against many temptations. It was an especially happy thought of Johnson's to write particular prayers for each of the major undertakings of his life, like the beginning of the *Dictionary* or the establishment of a new study. Thus he kept the connection between devotion and daily life.

It is a good thing that we are often with other people, for this is where our ministry is bound to lie. We are glad that our work takes us into homes and schools and towns and churches, because there is no Christianity without the fellowship. But it is likewise important to know the correlative truth that, for our life in the fellowship to be what it ought to be, there must also be some *aloneness*. Many today are never alone. Even when no other human being is present, they escape aloneness by turning on the radio or television or by using the telephone.

Actually, it can be very good to be alone and everyone needs some experience of this kind if he is to grow spiritually. If we are alone and do not resent the aloneness, wonderful growth can come accordingly. The very freedom from the necessity of making light conversation can sometimes be a truly great freedom. But we are not likely to have very much aloneness in the modern world unless we make it a conscious part of our discipline. It requires planning. The discipline of each individual Christian should include some time alone each day, for a brief period, and longer times alone, perhaps once a month. The latter is integral to the Kirkridge Discipline as developed by John Oliver Nelson and his companions. Perhaps we need, once a month, a private retreat of at least six hours. This is not easy to get in modern life, that strange life in which time-saving devices seem to leave us less time, but we may be able to get it if we realize sufficiently how valuable it is. At least it is a goal toward which we can aim.

Nearly all who attend a retreat and thereby experience, for the first time in their whole lives, the discipline of absolute freedom from conversation between the evening meeting and the next day's breakfast, are pathetically grateful for the experience. They have not realized, previously, what a relief it can be to prepare for bed and carry on one's personal devotions, both night and morning, without the necessity of engagement in small talk. It is a little thing, but because it is the beginning of a discipline, it is sometimes a great thing.

In conclusion, it may be necessary to say that there is no intrinsic conflict between Christian discipline and Christian joy. It is not only that discipline and joy are mutually consistent features of the Christian life; the deeper truth is that the acceptance of discipline leads to new joy. This is because the inner control, the new bondage, is the secret of perfect freedom.

THE ABOLITION OF THE LAITY

Some should be ... pastors and teachers for the equipment of the saints for the work of ministry.
EPHESIANS 4:11, 12

A quarter century ago the most commonly quoted remark of a contemporary Christian was the statement of Archbishop William Temple about the great new fact of our time. The great new fact, this wise man said, was the growing union in the churches. Undoubtedly the words were accurate when they were first spoken, but they would not be accurate if spoken now. Today we can still be grateful for the amount of church union that has been accomplished, but it is no longer novel and it is no longer the matter of first importance in Christian strategy. The great new fact in Christian experience today is the powerful drive in developing a universal ministry. We have made a brave start on the abolition of the laity, a movement according to which all who are Christians, whatever their particular gifts, must be engaged in some kind of ministry.

The old-fashioned idea, which we are now trying so hard to overcome, was the idea that religion is a professional matter. In spite of the current emphasis on lay religion there are people who, when they think of religion, immediately think of priests or clergymen or theologians. Religion, they

138

tend to suppose, is something that preachers have. If a man becomes deeply interested in the effort to make the gospel prevail, they begin to suspect that he has a professional stake in the religion business. There are people who leave religious discussion to their priests, much as they leave medical discussion to their physicians. Religion, then, is like medicine. There is a sense in which both are good for everybody, but they are dangerous in both instances, unless they are administered by those who have the professional stamp upon them. The very phrase "enter the church" has sometimes meant to become a clergyman. The lay member, of course, has his own responsibilities, but they are of a minor nature. Sometimes it seems that his major responsibilities are merely to add himself to the listening congregation and to give some money to support the work of the pastor.

It is obvious that there are many people who enjoy this sharp division of labor in the religious view; it is so much easier to sit in the balcony than to act on the stage. Life is far simpler if we are not required to participate. The layman who leaves all major responsibilities of the church to his pastor is really in a very comfortable position. He can tend to his secular business with very little interference from religious considerations. He can leave to the pastor, not only all of the preaching and praying, but also all of the visiting of new people. He is then free to criticize, if things are not well done, and he has an easy conscience because he has no important task in which it is possible to fail.

However comfortable and convenient this balcony view of the lay member has been, it is now conspicuously out of date and, in any case, betrays a complete misunderstanding of the nature of the Christian cause. Early Christianity was, for the most part, a movement in which the distinction between clergy and laity was utterly unknown. Indeed, our

139

conventional distinction between clerical and lay Christians does not appear anywhere in the entire New Testament. There was, at first, nothing which even approached the separated priesthood. The distinction broke down on both sides. On what we might call the professional side, it broke down because a man like Paul worked with his own hands. "For you remember our labor and toil, brethren; we worked night and day, that we might not burden any of you, while we preached to you the gospel of God" (I Thess. 2:9). On what we are tempted to call the lay side, ordinary men and women worked mightily to extend Christ's Kingdom. Early Christianity won against great odds, not primarily because it had a few brilliant leaders, but far more because the idea of a nonministering Christian seems to have been rejected unanimously. *The mood was not so much anti-clerical as anti-lay.* Insofar as we are trying to abolish the laity, we are, in essence, trying to recapture the mood of first-century Christianity.

One of the most creative features of the early Christian pattern was the clear understanding of the relationship that existed between a pastor or teacher on the one hand, and an ordinary member on the other. This relationship is perfectly expressed in the classic statement of our text, from the fourth chapter of Ephesians. Some men, it was recognized, had special gifts in guiding others in that they could counsel and teach. This is not surprising, for it is ever so, in any generation. Some people are especially gifted as teachers, just as others are especially gifted in administration or some other ability. What is important is the *purpose* of this particular kind of ministry.

The purpose of a good pastor, whatever his means of financial support may be, is to make the universal ministry succeed. More and more this is what pastors must be taught to do. The powers of each member must be watched lovingly and an effort made to develop these powers to the fullest possible extent. There is no room, in such a conception, for a mere audience. The person who resists participation in all forms of ministry has not yet discovered what the true meaning of the Christian faith is.

Now that the idea of the universal ministry is beginning to be well accepted, our next task is that of developing concrete, practical teaching about the forms that the ministry of ordinary saints can take. One of the best of these forms is that of the ministry of books. Some business and professional men now see the distribution of books as their finest opportunity. They are aware that our time is marked by the production of a great deal of strong and persuasive Christian writing, but they are also aware that very little of this reaches the minds of the rank and file in the local churches. Therefore a man may feel called to buy several copies of a book that has opened new doors in his own life and to carry some of these about with him in the course of his regular work. Let us say, for example, that *Letters to Young Churches* by J. B. Phillips has given him a new and vivid understanding of the early church, by putting the New Testament Epistles into the language of our day. The next step is to hand the translation to as many of his acquaintances as are prepared to appreciate it. Ministry of such a practical character can be performed without offense. The carrier of the book can simply say, "This volume has meant much to me; perhaps it will mean the same to you." What often results is a chain reaction in which the recipient next becomes the giver or lender. The same can be done with inexpensive pamphlets such as those now put out by the Upper Room and many other publishing organizations. We do not lack materials; what we lack is enough people who will provide

141

the chief means by which one good thing is ever passed on to another.

Some, who now are serious about the universal ministry, can volunteer to conduct book tables within their church buildings, particularly on Sunday mornings. One who is willing to undertake this ministry can place a table in some part of the building, where people naturally pass by, and thus a wholly new group is reached. Curious as it may seem, not many people buy books or even know how to do so. There are large towns without bookstores and, though the denominational book services are active, people do not ordinarily buy books unless they actually see them in front of their eyes. To encourage people to buy is much better than to loan from a library, because then the book a man owns may be loaned to others. Furthermore he may mark it and thus make it truly his own.

There need be no fear that the selling of books at church will introduce a jarring commercial note. There is nothing wrong with money, from a Christian point of view, especially when it is used to spread Christ's Kingdom. There is no difference, in principle, between the collection of money, in an offering, in order to spread the gospel to foreign lands and the collection of money from buyers of Christian books, in order to increase the spread of Christian ideas in the minds of the buyers. Both operations are part of the missionary enterprise. All suspicion of wrong motive can be allayed by carrying on the operation on a nonprofit basis. In any case, it is increasingly true that the steady operation of a book table, week after week, is one of the marks of a truly aroused church. The operation need not burden the pastor at all, and will not burden him, if some lay man or woman accepts the responsibility. Often willing people come to a pastor to ask for suggestions about what they can do. This is one.

Another suggestion which holds real promise is that of the conduct of a coffee hour on Sunday morning. Because the discussion of ideas over cups of coffee is a gracious modern practice, there is no good reason why the church should not employ it. The cost is slight in comparison with the human value, the chief value consisting in the way in which the institution helps members and attenders to know one another. Those who have a vision of this, and are willing to manage the details, are making a real, though modest, contribution to church life.

Many other forms of universal ministry occur to us when we begin to use our minds. The practice of introducing the lay reader into the conduct of public worship has many advantages, one of them being the good relationship which it tends to produce between the pastor and the reader. In most cases it is good for the pastor to train the reader during the week before the reading occurs, and this time together tends to become a valuable bond. The common result is that the reading is done with such comprehension that it frequently is far superior to reading done by professionals, who suppose that they need no special practice.

Increasingly, the ministry which the ordinary member performs best, once he is trained, is that of visiting families. Visiting is a skill to be learned like any other skill, and can sometimes be done more successfully by a member than by a professional pastor. This is because the pastor's call is seen by many as something in his line of duty, for which he is paid. When he comes, he is simply doing what he is supposed to do, but the visits of ordinary saints are likely to be seen in a totally different light. In many areas of experience the member has advantages over the professional, chiefly because his contributions are not automatically discounted. The pastor says good things, some suppose, because it is his business to say them, but the layman's message comes as a surprise and is therefore accepted at its full value.

An encouraging example of the use of creative imagination in developing the ministry of calling is provided by a Methodist church in an Ohio city, in which, under the pastor's careful leadership, there has been organized a Guild of St. Andrew, made up of twenty-four dedicated men. These men, who represent a number of businesses and professions, gather for a light supper each Thursday evening and go out after supper to visit families. Before they go out, the men receive instruction from their pastor and then proceed two by two, after the fashion of the Seventy as described in the tenth chapter of Luke's gospel. The men do not go at random, but carry on their visits in a planned manner, with some advance knowledge of the homes to which they are assigned and with some idea of what to say. When the visits are completed, the members of the Guild return to the church building, where they report to one another on their successes and their failures. Nearly always, they learn not only from their own firsthand experience, but also from the experiences of others.

A variation on this experiment is found in the recruitment of a "New Seventy." These are deeply grounded men and women who are willing, with the pastor's guidance, to take specific responsibilities for specific individuals and families. The most common method is for each member of this responsible group to watch carefully over five others. His task is not only to see that these people are visited, but also that they are provided with helpful magazines and books and even transportation when this is required. Each one of the Seventy helps his five people in their personal religious devotion, in problems of family worship, and in the religious education of the children. When seriously tried, this produces really remarkable results and has, in some cases, revived an entire church. It would be impossible for one pastor to give really adequate care to three hundred and fifty people, but it is not at all impossible for seventy truly committed people to accomplish this result. The secret of such advance lies in the process of multiplication rather than mere addition. The gifted pastor does not do all the work himself, but by liberating the lay forces, multiplies the available resources.

Modern churches are often so complex in organization that they tend to need business managers. The standard solution is for the pastor himself to become such a manager, but this is often a shame. It is a shame because the pastor is thereby enticed away from his more prophetic duties. The result is that the pastors become hectic men, more familiar with mimeograph machines than with great books, and more adept at money raising than at helping people with their personal devotional development.

What is the solution of this pressing problem? It is obvious that we cannot reverse the process and return to the simplicity once known. Modern churches must have offices and budgets and these require administrators. The solution lies in the lay ministry. Persons who have ability in business management must come forward as volunteers to take over these duties and thus set the pastors free. It is not very important whether this is done with payment or without. That depends wholly on what the financial needs of each volunteer are. Much can be done by volunteer secretaries and bookkeepers and those who have special abilities in looking after physical properties. Once this vision is really caught, the pastor becomes a liberated and, consequently, a far more productive man, the members meanwhile learning the joys of participation in the total redemptive enterprise.

Most Protestants are rank amateurs in the development

of general participation, when compared to the Mormons. The latter expect every man to give at least a year of his life, preferably in early maturity, as a missionary for the church at his own expense. But, important as this general ministry is, the Mormons do not stop there. When they completed the building of their new temple in Los Angeles they allowed the general public to visit the building for several weeks prior to dedication. Members in the area served in shifts of about forty persons, for four or five hours at a time, acting as information officers and guides. This was a wonderful idea, for it accomplished several purposes at once. Not only did it make an excellent impression upon the visitors, most of whom were non-Mormons; it also did something for the volunteer workers who came to feel more and more that they were part of the undertaking which they were assigned to explain. It was wise to use about eighty different persons each day and thus spread widely the sense of participation which the opening of the new building made possible.

It is not always the case that such fine opportunities arise, but the shame is that we often miss the ones we do have. Some of us would have been foolish enough, in the face of an opportunity like that of the Los Angeles Mormons, to use staff to do the work. Sometimes we hire singers to entertain us on Sunday mornings! The temptation to solve problems by adding to the paid staff, illustrating some aspects of Parkinson's Law, in most cases must be resisted, if possible. Even when the holders of office are not paid, there is a real danger of allowing individuals to have vested interests in official positions. Lay people can be quite as much in love with ecclesiastical power as clergymen ever are. The solution is to institute the practice of rotation in office so that new life is always being used. The greatest evil which comes, when a few monopolize offices, is the failure to use powers which are, in consequence, undeveloped. What we seek is a kind of life in which all feel like members of the crew and not part of the passenger list. The church is a ship which has no places for mere passengers, because all of the places are taken by those pulling at the oars. There is no other way to make the ship go.

As we move out into the great new day of the gospel which is now before us, the hope is that the idea of the lay Apostolate or the universal ministry may become generally accepted. We shall all be ministers and we shall all be laymen at the same time, for *laos* means "The whole people of God." Minister and layman are thus two ways of denoting the same person. But the acceptance of this idea is bound to involve serious new responsibilities, the chief of which is the training for a new kind of ministry.

The new fact of our time leads directly to the necessity of a new form of education. As long as lay men and women are satisfied to be passive observers in the Christian movement, leaving the real leadership and the vocal witness to the professional clergyman, the education of the rank and file of Christians, though a desirable end, is not really urgent. But the moment Christian housewives and Christian businessmen come to feel a greater measure of responsibility for the conduct of the Christian cause, the problem of education is urgent indeed. It is not enough that men should speak or write; it is important that they speak or write the truth, insofar as this is humanly possible. A far greater Christianity may emerge if there is a universal, instead of a restricted ministry, but the greater vitality comes at a high price, the price of new problems. If we want to keep our problems fewer and simpler, we are wise to stay by the more conventional and more timid pattern.

147

The Sunday School, as presently understood, will not suffice. It will not suffice chiefly because the time available is too short and because the atmosphere of serious study cannot normally be produced. What we shall need, before we are through, is a great many layman's seminaries. Is it not an amazing fact that, in a country predominantly Protestant, upholding for years the doctrine of the priesthood of the believer, there should be scores of theological seminaries for professional clergy, but not one primarily for lay men and women? Some day, as men look back, this failure will seem almost incomprehensible. Lay people may not be able to give the extended or continuous time to theological study which is given by those preparing for the pastorate, but they should have the opportunity of studying the same subjects with equal seriousness. Some already have proved, by individual effort, that they can study with equal success. Fortunately, there is in the Christian religion no realm of esoteric or secret study. The great themes of God, of God's word, of Christ's revelation, of Christian history and Christian thought are such that any really interested and competent person, whatever his secular occupation, can pursue them.

If we build lay seminaries, they will necessarily have a pattern different from what has been known in the seminaries of the past. Arrangements must be made for people to come when they can, often for short periods. Much can be done in evenings and much in vacation periods. Many will have to go forward on the basis of independent study and many others by correspondence. Difficulties there are, and further difficulties there will be, but we dare not let these hinder us unduly.

Though the establishment of lay seminaries is a matter of urgency, we need not wait for these, because we have an excellent resource ready at hand, if only we are willing to employ it. This resource is that of the use of the local pastor as a theological teacher. We have thousands of gifted and theologically trained men who are qualified to train lay ministers right in the local community. There is no good reason why a well-educated pastor should not spend a large share of his time in a scholarly way, teaching one night a course in Christian Classics and another night a course in the Philosophy of Religion.

There are some places in which this is done and very well done, and the results are sometimes revolutionary, but the amazing thing is that it is done so seldom. When we try to think why the pattern is so rare we are really mystified and have no adequate answer. It cannot be because the pastors are unable to teach—that is what they are trained to do. A man who has studied for three years, with a scholarly approach to the Bible ought certainly to be able to give a one-year course with the same approach. It cannot be for lack of time. After all, the pastor, more than most men, is the master of his own time, and, though human demands are numerous, he can always work on a system of priorities. The failure to carry on serious theological teaching cannot arise from the unwillingness of the potential lay ministers to study. The amazing success of the Great Books Movement and the phenomenal growth in all adult education show how eager the people are, once they are given the opportunity.

We are therefore driven to the conclusion that the relative paucity of experiments in adult theological education arises merely from a lack of imagination. Because it has not been a part of the dominant pattern of the recent religious past, it does not occur to us. But, once it does occur to us, the pattern may change radically. Herein lies hope. If each church should begin to be a small local theological seminary, incalculable changes may come in a generation.

149

THE MINISTRY OF DAILY WORK

We must work the works of him who sent me, while it is day; night comes, when no one can work. JOHN 9:4

Though the contemporary emphasis on the ministry of ordinary Christians leads to a number of valuable contributions in connection with the ongoing work of the church, the greatest single ministry in which most men can engage is that which occurs in the pursuit of their regular employment. God may care more about factories and offices than about church buildings, because more people are in them more of the time. It matters very little how effective a man may be in teaching a class at church or in leading a prayer meeting, if he is not able to make the same kind of witness carry over to the people who work with him every day. The problem of how our ministry may rightly be performed in the midst of our daily toil is a problem of such importance that we need to enlist, in our effort to solve it, all of the help that we can get from one another. Even after we have learned all that we can, we shall not know enough.

One reason for the great importance of the subject consists in the fact that a great many people care deeply about the work that they do. Sometimes they care so deeply about their work that they like shoptalk better than conversation on any other subject and are comparatively miserable when, because of illness or some other reason, they are deprived of participation in their work. There are wholly credible stories, therefore, of men who spend their days off, going to see the people who are substituting for them. Often the difficulties encountered in sudden retirement are merely an index of the meaning which work had come to have over a period of years.

Because of his love of employment a man's work may become an effective handle by means of which he may be reached. If we are wise we shall recognize this and make use of it in the Christian cause. Already we can point to men who have shown that, though they could not be reached by some general appeal to all men, they could be reached when appealed to specifically as lawyers or engineers or physicians or professors. Long ago, in the formation of the Gideon Society, the point was demonstrated that men could be reached mightily if approached as Christian traveling salesmen. Because they were salesmen they decided to do something to reach other salesmen and, accordingly, began to put Bibles into hotel rooms all over the land. The life of common "drummers" was thus dignified. More recently, similar efforts have succeeded among professional soldiers, athletes, and several other vocational groups. So successful is this approach that we are beginning to dream of great new developments in what may eventually be known as "vocational evangelism." If it is true, as it is, that a physician is attracted to a Christian Doctor's group, when he has never been involved in any Christian society previously, and if we learn that this has occurred because he has come to a new sense of the connection between his beloved vocation and the gospel, this is a very important fact. There is no telling how far this emphasis may lead us. Of one such study group a doctor writes, "It is now possible to say that these men, in

151

busy active practice, are now meeting their problems and their patients under a Judeo-Christian ethic."

While it is true that an opportunity is presented in the lives of people who honor what they do, it is also true that we must find some way of reaching millions who hate their work every day of their lives. All of us know a great many persons who would not toil at their present jobs a single day, if only they could be relieved of the burdensome responsibility of supporting themselves and their families. Going to work is a bitter task and leaving it is a daily release. Many feel that what they are doing has no special or unique relationship to their abilities and that the entire connection is a matter of accident or convenience. Why, a man asks, am I selling vacuum cleaners or dispensing gasoline or serving as a cashier in the bank? Living in another community, at a different time, I might have done something else. And why not? Perhaps I shall, he says, do something else next year. After all, one job is not much worse than another.

In addition to this general difficulty, there is, as everyone knows, the added contemporary difficulty of the trivialization of jobs through increased mechanization. This is a problem which has become worse with each increasing year and will become still worse before it is better. As the processes of industrialization spread to all the globe, the same problem will finally be met everywhere. It will be felt in Nairobi and Monrovia, as it is now felt in Detroit and Birmingham. We have gained much, in our standard of living, from the fact that cars and refrigerators can be made swiftly, but the inevitable price of such swift production is that some man may have to stand all day, putting a screw in the same part of each door that comes by. The question, which we have not answered fully, and which we may never answer in a really satisfactory way, is how this man can find dignity in his work.

It is easy to talk with the physician about the dignity of *his* work, because he may be able to point to children who now run and skip with laughter, instead of riding in wheel chairs, because he diagnosed polio in time. That kind of work is self-authenticating, as is also the work of the teacher, the pastor, the nurse and many more, but how does this apply to the man assembling the refrigerator door?

Perhaps the worst that can be said of an increasing number of jobs, as fewer of our people work on the land, and more work in factories, is not that jobs are too difficult, but that they are too easy to enable men to build up self-respect. In a short time the requisite skill is learned and then there is nothing but repetition of what a man comes to believe could be done almost as well by a child. The man is mechanized because his labor seems trivial. He can still get satisfaction from his family, his church, his labor union, his club, but it seems almost impossible to find satisfaction in that to which he gives the greater share of his waking hours.

One paradoxical result of this situation, in which men hate and despise their work, is that their hours of leisure tend to become almost as meaningless as their hours of employment. One might suppose that a man who hates his job would be determined that at least his free hours would be full of meaning, but often it turns out the other way. The man is so fed up with his job that he dashes from it into anything that can make him forget, with the result that he spends his free time in the saloon or in passive watching of television, with no creative life of his own at all. Some grasp the opportunity for craftsmanship or advanced education or good reading or co-operative tasks with their children, but the sad truth is that a great many seem never to move in such directions at all. The emptiness of their employment is matched by the emptiness of their freedom from employment. It is at such points as this that the gospel must be brought to bear, if it is to be truly relevant to our time.

Man is so made that he can never live well without a sense of meaning. If meaning is absent very long, something terrible is likely to occur, as it occurred in Germany under the evil, but understandable, influence of Hitler. The chief ways in which most people can ever show meaning in their little lives is through their daily work and through their families. These are where we are likely to make a difference if we make a difference at all. One of the surest ways to destroy a man is to force him to do something that is intentionally trivial and meaningless, as has sometimes been done in military punishment. The classic example is of the man forced to dig a hole exactly six feet long, six feet wide, and six feet deep, with perfectly squared and plumb corners, knowing all the time that, as soon as his work is complete and has passed meticulous inspection, he will be told to fill the hole. Not many human beings could stand this very long without going mad.

Once, during the Great Depression, a farmer in Virginia brought into town a load of beautiful potatoes which he had produced, with pride, on his farm. The government purchasing agent weighed the potatoes and then said, "Now we shall pour kerosene on them and burn them." "No, you won't," said the farmer. He felt that the whole thing was an insult, a way of ridiculing his careful labor. Kerosene would have helped burn poor potatoes as efficiently as good ones, and the support price would have been the same in either case. Consequently the farmer recovered his potatoes from the buyer, and sold them to the A & P store at a lower price. Some people, as a result, were able to purchase potatoes more cheaply than they could otherwise have done, but the farmer's self-respect was preserved.

Much of the glory of human life comes as we are conscious partners in creation. It is in this fashion, more than in any other, that we verify our position as creatures made in God's image. Since God is the Infinite Creator, the way to show that we are made in His image is to become finite creators. We leave the world with a house or a book or an invention or a painting or a church or a factory that would never have existed, in all of eternity, apart from our toil or imagination or persistence. No enduring happiness comes in any other way. The man who knows that he is a parasite cannot but be miserable. This is the brilliantly expressed philosophy of Exupéry in *Wind, Sand and Stars*.

It is only when we become conscious of our part in life, however modest, that we shall be happy. Only then will we be able to live in peace and die in peace, for only this lends meaning to life and death.

We are clear, then, about our clue, though we feel extremely inadequate when it comes to the ability to apply it. There is at least one thing which we can say to the man who turns the screw in the door of the refrigerator. We can tell him that such machines are needed to make life better for men and women and little children. People are better off if their food is kept fresh by refrigeration. Moreover, if we are to have such instruments, men must make them, and it is uneconomical for one man to try to make one alone. We must work in teamwork if we are to survive at the present level of population. Therefore every item in the work is necessary. The man who puts in the smallest part is needed because, without this part, the total undertaking would not be complete. Of course the work is dull, but parts of every known job are dull. We establish ourselves as participating in the creative process by our joyous and uncomplaining willing-

155

ness to perform tasks which are trivial in themselves, because they are necessary for the whole.

This may not be much to say, but it is something! And we do not really know anything else to say. The sermon on that topic is inevitably short.

What is increasingly hopeful is the realization that many tasks involve far more opportunities than we at first expect to find. A good example is that of work of an industrial manager. We tend to think of him, in caricature, as hard bitten and hard driving, concerned only with showing profit on the books of the company, but, in actual experience, the manager may well be a man with untold opportunities of a personal nature. There is, in one American city, a plant in which two hundred persons are employed, every one of whom is known personally to the manager, who becomes a kind of pastor. He advises them about their financial problems, about their family troubles, about the future education of their children. In fact, this manager has spiritual opportunities which the pastor of a church might well envy. Perhaps the time will come when the idea of manager as pastor will be generally accepted. If it is, the church can do wonders in bringing Christian managers together in a vocational society, so that each can be strengthened by the others and all can learn from each other.

Another good example of opportunity which is real, but easily missed, is seen in the career of a man who is a pharmacist. This man, after coming out of military service in 1945, began to work consciously toward his goal of having a pharmacy of his own and of putting it on a high professional level by dispensing nothing but prescriptions and sickroom supplies. He was proud of being a pharmacist, an auxiliary part of the healing enterprise, and he wanted his work to illustrate its inherent dignity. It took the man a long time to get started, because at first he had no money and he had to work for others while he saved. Finally he reached the place where he was able to begin, with the narrowest conceivable margin of financial safety. It was a struggle, and twice he suffered robbery, but he won his battle and is now secure in his success, with six employees of his own.

Not long ago this man made what seems to many to be a strange addition to his career. He was beginning to search for his ministry in common life and he found it in the decision to help another pharmacist to start from nothing. Accordingly he went to another town, rented quarters, stocked a pharmacy at his own expense, and gave a younger pharmacist a chance to operate it, with a guaranteed income until the new man could get on his feet. When asked what he would do if this venture should succeed, he said, "Why, I'll start another." He went on to point out that, in his philosophy of the Christian religion, a man who is fortunate dare not let the chain reaction stop with him. If it ends there the whole story is pathetic. There is always some way in which it can be passed to another.

A third relevant illustration is of the part which a local pastor recently played in regard to a man's employment. The employee came to the pastor several times, over a period of weeks, to tell of a moral problem. The man had stolen a few items from the shop where he worked and this worried him terribly. He wished to take them back, but there was no way in which he could do so without detection, and the inflexible rule of the factory was that theft led to suspension. A new arrangement was in effect, according to which the cars of the workers could no longer be parked close to the mill and this made inconspicuous return of the property practically impossible. Finally the pastor worked out a bold plan. Having good reason to believe that the parishioner was sincerely penitent, the pastor went, alone, to the manager of the factory, who was entirely willing to see him. The pastor, without disclosing the identity of the penitent man, told the story and offered to bring back the stolen property in his own hands. The manager accepted the plan, the welfare of the worker's family was not harmed and all goes well. But this occurred because a pastor realized that much of his best service bears on man's toil.

With these concrete illustrations in mind we may be able to help ourselves or others to find a new glory in common work. Every work has people in it, and, as long as there are people, there are opportunities for the Christian ministry. What we must always resist is the blasphemous notion that our work is just a job. Though it is difficult to achieve, the task of each son and daughter of God is to find the calling for which each was made. If we do not find it at first, we ought to try again. It is a great shame to waste the only earthly life we shall ever live. The task of the Christian ministry is to turn all work into vocation.

A real step forward in the recognition of the Christian significance of daily work has been made recently in the dedication of some of the beautiful new church buildings which have been constructed. The heart of the idea is that the dedication is an opportunity to recognize and to glorify the work which plumbers, painters, carpenters, and bricklayers have done. Each group is recognized in turn and God is thanked for their labor. The fine new building thus becomes a means by which some dignity is brought into otherwise modest lives. Here is a glimpse of the frontier to which the gospel brings us when we begin to understand what it means.

The function of the Christian faith, in regard to the machine, is not to fight the machine, but to try to dignify the lives of the men and women who use machines and the products of machines. Whenever possible, we must encourage the development of work in which people can take pride in what they do because of the beauty or the utility of their productions. Excellent illustrations of how this can be done are provided by the Corning Glass Works of Corning, New York, and by the Wedgwood factory, near Stoke-on-Trent, in England. In both of these establishments, and in many more, workers are encouraged, partly by the presence of admiring visitors, to enjoy the achievement of excellence. A man who designs a Wedgwood plate is paid in something besides money. More and more, as committed Christians find themselves in positions in which they can make a difference, much of their ministry will consist in guiding industrial development in this direction. The Christian is not only a person who becomes a partner with God in creation; he is also a person who tries to help other people to do the same. There is no finer work than that by means of which we help others to see the dignity of their own work.

A
FAITH
FOR
SCIENTISTS

You shall love the Lord your God . . . with all your mind. LUKE 10:27

It is a mistake to suppose that the Christian religion is primarily interested in what goes on in churches. The gospel by its very nature must be concerned with all of life and all of experience. This is because God is the sovereign Lord of all days and not merely of days set aside for worship. Religion is concerned with how men think, with how they play, with how they marry, with how they work, and with how they die. One of the most fruitful of all teachings is that of the sacramental view of the world. This teaching is, essentially, that physical things can be the means by which God's glory is revealed and that the right use of physical things is a religious duty. Christianity has spiritual aspects, but it is far from being a merely spiritual religion. This is the fundamental reason why the Christian faith is deeply concerned with contemporary science.

The burden which society lays upon contemporary scientists is great and it will be greater. The public interest in science, both pure and applied, is now so keen and the public dismay, when failure occurs, is so vocal, that the ordinary scientist, whether he likes it or not, is cast in a new role. He is now a public servant, with all of the privileges and dangers

160

which such service entails. To a degree never before necessary, the scientist needs to understand himself and his vocation.

Great burdens, if they are to be carried well, require great resources. More and more the problem of the practicing scientist is, accordingly, the problem of the faith which sustains him. It is not enough, at any time, to be concerned only with the particular laboratory task, since every task implies larger issues, but the necessity of concern about general convictions is now obvious to all who think about the matter, and it is especially obvious to scientists themselves.

All science is based ultimately upon faith. To suppose that science simply begins by inquiring, wholly without presuppositions, is to be naïve indeed. For one thing, all scientific work, including all experimentation, rests upon moral foundations. Science, as we know it, would be quite impossible apart from a tremendous and overarching concern for honesty. A true scientist, giving his pet theory the most searching analysis of which he is capable, is as zealous in watching for negative as for positive evidence. We can go further and say truly that a genuine scientist is one who is always trying to disprove his own hypothesis. In this sense many, who have never worked in laboratories, are scientists in spirit. If ever this strong moral basis decays, science itself will decay, no matter how clever the gadgets and no matter how palatial the laboratories.

In addition to this moral basis, there is a still deeper foundation of the scientific enterprise. This is the conviction, which no one has ever proved, that our world is fundamentally orderly and essentially dependable. It must be carefully noted that our faith in this regard goes far beyond the fact. Even if we find the world dependable in the little area which we have observed, that does not prove that it is dependable in the vast area so far unobserved, by us or by anyone else, and it does not prove that it will be dependable tomorrow. Because the future is not yet, we therefore do not know, with certainty, what events it will demonstrate or what laws they will obey. Our fundamental and necessary faith, however, is that events will continue to obey laws of the kind which rational minds like ours can contemplate and partly understand. Our faith necessarily involves the conviction that the laws of the world are somehow akin to the laws of thought. Not all scientists realize that they are actually operating in the light of such a faith, but their realization increases as they go beyond the superficial aspects of their work.

Since faith is necessary for science, or even for living, it is important to try to understand what faith means. There are always some, of course, who suppose that faith belongs to the prescientific mentality or that it is opposed to reason. They think, as they relive the intellectual battles of their childhood, that faith is the same as credulity—that it is an effort to believe what we have good reason to doubt or even to deny. If that is what faith means, it is not worth discussing, much less defending. The scientist, with the heavy burdens of our day upon him, will not be helped by any kind of obscurantism.

Faith, in the great tradition of Western man, involves an element of belief, but it transcends belief, and is more closely akin to trust. Faith is not belief in the face of negative evidence, but trust in the light of abundant, though not complete, positive evidence. *Faith is trust in a fundamental meaningfulness which is not wholly proved and presumably will not be wholly proved in our finite existence, but which makes more sense out of our puzzling world than does any conceivable alternative.* Instead of denying evidence, faith seeks to bring the available evidence into a meaningful pattern. It is a major conviction which can bring order to nearly all of the minor and fragmentary convictions. Faith is not something which dispels all the darkness, but it is a brave gamble on the brightest light we see. "Faith," said Professor Kirsopp Lake, "is not belief in spite of evidence, but life in scorn of consequences."

If all men need faith, and if scientists need it with especial urgency, it is highly important to be selective in our faith. Not just any faith will do. Some faiths are obviously more nearly adequate than others are. There are faiths which degrade human life and there are faiths which ennoble it. Perhaps the best intellectual procedure is to try to see what the criteria of an adequate faith are.

No faith will suffice which does not recognize that our knowledge is extremely fragmentary. We know very little about the external world or even about ourselves, and the truth is that we have not done so well. We need a faith which involves the great truth that man, whatever his achievements, is not the master of his fate. No faith will suffice if it merely bolsters man's pride; it must also make him recognize his wretchedness.

We seek, likewise, a faith which transcends the experience of the moment. A central conviction is worth very little unless it refers to that which endures. No faith is adequate which refers only to our little time. It must include, in its purview, the long ages before the advent of man and the long ages after human life on this earth is gone. An adequate faith must refer, not merely to time, but to eternity. If anything is sure, it is that all of us will die. A faith to live by must also be a faith by which a man can die.

All men have many sides to their lives, and in this regard scientists are no exception. We need a faith, therefore, which can include, in its total scope, what can be demonstrated in

163

laboratories and what cannot be demonstrated there. It would be absurd to stress the astronomy and to forget the astronomer. Actually it is easy to forget, in our public interest in science, that there is no science without scientists and that scientists are men. Each physicist or chemist or rocket expert is a person, with all of the difficulties and dangers of other persons. Most scientists have families; all lose those who are dearest to them; many are members of churches; many are men of prayer; most of them accept their responsibilities as citizens and makers of public opinion. The basic question is not whether we can launch earth satellites, but rather what kind of life we propose to lead. The answers to such questions come, not from technology of any kind, but from basic convictions about value and meaning.

Furthermore, the only faith worth having is an honest faith. There are undoubtedly areas of reality to which our rationality never fully penetrates, but we dare not be antirational. To every faith we must apply the known tests of rational coherence. We cannot respect a man, be he scientist or layman, who lives his life in compartments, which are logically incompatible with one another. We cannot honor a man who, by his doctrine, undercuts all possibility of logical discourse, and at the same time tries to use logic to support his own position. A man may adopt any positon he cares to espouse, but it is required of him that at the same time he accept, without equivocation, the further positions which his original position implies. He connot honestly talk in terms of value, if his central faith makes the idea of value meaningless. A devout man accepts the rules of logic.

There may be more criteria than these, but together they set a very high standard. We shall have made a brave beginning if we find a faith which is marked by *humility, permanence, wholeness,* and intellectual *integrity*. A religion which is relevant will help us to find or to produce a faith which can meet such tests.

The good news is that such a faith is already in existence, that it transcends our denominational differences, and that it is more wonderful than we ordinarily know. Though it has frequently been overlaid and partially lost, it is really a thing of wonder. It is centered in the conviction that the Living God truly is, that this world, with all its confusion, is His world, that He has a purpose for it, and that we, in spite of our sin and ignorance, are actually made in His image. Perhaps no one has ever stated this central faith better than did Blaise Pascal three hundred years ago. The God, in whose objective reality the faith of millions of thoughtful men is centered, said Pascal, "is not a God who is simply the author of mathematical truths, or of the order of the elements. . . . He is not merely a God who exercises His providence over the lives and fortunes of men, to bestow on those who worship Him a long and happy life. . . . But the God of Abraham, the God of Isaac, the God of Jacob, the God of Christians, is a God of love and comfort, a God who fills the soul and heart of those whom He possesses, a God who makes them conscious of their inmost inward wretchedness, and His infinite mercy, who unites Himself to their inmost soul, who fills it with humility and joy, with confidence and love, who renders them incapable of any other end than Himself." (*Pensées*, 555.)

Here is a faith which meets all of the tests which have been suggested:

In the first place it produces genuine humility. The faith in the Living God makes us know that God's world is bigger and older than anything we can make. It was God, not ourselves, who made the world and its laws, which we belatedly and poorly ascertain. We are filled with wonder at the realization that God has made one known creature, ourselves, in His image, in the sense that we alone, of all created things, experience some genuine freedom and can, consequently, share in creation. God is wholly free, but our freedom is limited; God is completely personal, but we are partly personal; we see through a glass darkly, but God sees face to face. Some day we may know as we are known, but not now. The classic faith, while it gives immense meaning to life, never makes men proud, for it insists, with equal force, upon the greatness of man and the littleness of man. God has not sought us because we are worthy, but in spite of our unworthiness.

The classic faith provides, in the second place, a rational conviction which involves trust in what is permanent. The conviction is that God's purpose, in seeking to make finite creatures who can be really free, has been engaged in this task from the foundations of the world, and will continue in all eternity. What we see in this life is only a fragment of the Divine Purpose, which undoubtedly is bigger than we can know. The purpose of God is longer and bigger than we can even think, in that "the sufferings of the present time are not worthy to be compared with the glory which shall be revealed to us" (Rom. 8:18). The fact that "the glorious liberty of the children of God" is not perfectly demonstrated on this earth is no final answer; there is the reality of life everlasting.

Compare the grandeur of this faith with the position of the scientific humanist, whose faith is now seen to be even more inadequate than before. There is no evidence that humanity is permanent. Not only is it likely to come to an end, with the increase of entropy; it may, in the light of present possibilities, come to an end much sooner. It is now widely believed, on good authority, that man at last has the capacity to destroy himself as a race. Those who are humanists, and no more, are understandably sad in the light of this prospect. They have nothing enduring on which to stake their faith. Faith in progress becomes a feeble thing in the light of modern events. Consequently these people are today among the most frightened of men. How different their outlook would be if they could appreciate and believe the noble words with which the eighth chapter of Romans concludes:

For I am persuaded, that neither death, nor life, nor angels, nor principalities, nor powers, nor things present, nor things to come, nor height nor depth nor any other creature, shall be able to separate us from the love of God, which is in Christ Jesus our Lord.

While the faith of the humanist faces eventual and complete defeat, in the destruction of the human race which is wholly alien to the world which spawns it, this is not true of the faith in the God of Abraham, Isaac, and Jacob, the Father of Jesus Christ. In this larger faith destruction can be faced with remarkable equanimity. Of course this world, the Bible teaches, may be rolled up as a scroll. Why should we expect it to be otherwise? William Shakespeare was expressing the major Christian conviction about the essential transitoriness of all physical things when, in *The Tempest*, he wrote the words which appear, in connection with his statue, in the Poets' Corner of Westminster Abbey:

> *The cloud capp'd towers, the gorgeous palaces,*
> *The solemn temples, the great globe itself,*
> *Yea, all which it inherit, shall dissolve,*
> *And, like this insubstantial pageant faded,*
> *Leave not a rack behind.*

The world is dependent upon God, but the logical relation is not reversible; God is not dependent upon the created world.

167

He could make another in the twinkling of an eye. Here we have no continuing city, but that fact alone does not bring real sadness to the believer. At best, this world is a place of preparation and hope, rather than a place of fulfillment. All of the injustices we experience here can be rectified in the Life Everlasting. It is no wonder that the faith is one which causes men to *sing*.

In the third place, the classic faith speaks to the whole man. The faith, as known in the prophetic tradition, is concerned with both minds and bodies, for it recognizes both the spiritual and the material orders at the same time. Far from neglecting bodies, the faith has been the chief inspiration in human history for the establishment of hospitals to aid in healing bodies and in projects for the feeding of the hungry. Always there is a temptation to stress only one side of the human situation, whether intellectual or physical or spiritual, but the faith has resisted this temptation. It has been concerned with people in families, with people in laboratories, with people at prayer, and with people in spiritual need. The power of the prophetic faith has consisted, not in its ability to draw men out of common life, but in its ability to impart to common life both dignity and meaning.

Much honest faith fails at the point of wholeness because it is centered in some abstraction such as a system of natural law. The difficulty here is that the very richness of experience, which most needs to be accounted for, is left wholly unexplained. Christ, in the opening words of His most unforgettable prayer, unites with marvelous simplicity the grandeur of the far-flung physical world and the deeply personal character of its Author. Christ showed that He combined both awe and intimate trust when he said, "I thank thee, Father, Lord of heaven and earth" (Matt. 11:25). It is only in the person that we find wholeness, including both awareness and objective reference. The classic faith meets the test of wholeness better than does any other because it is rooted in faith in the Infinite Person.

A fourth mark of the adequacy of theistic faith is that it can meet the tests of intellectual integrity. The great tradition is not that of men who believe in the Living God and His purpose for them, because such belief is comforting, but that of men who believe because there is evidence that it is true. The notion that God has a plan for your life is in many ways an inconvenient belief. Obviously it limits self-indulgence. There may be some who espouse a faith as a result of wishful thinking, but the far more profound observation is that of Pascal, that men "fear it is true."

It is doubtful if any single influence has been more productive of the life of reason than has the faith in the Living God. All who know anything of our intellectual history are bound to be impressed with the fact that nearly all of modern science, in America, was for years nourished chiefly in institutions founded and supported by churches. Most of our original colleges were church colleges and these became scientific centers. This is no accident. The faith, when it understands itself, is bound to be the enemy of all intellectual dishonesty. Insofar as science means following the evidence where it leads, it is the natural product of faith in the Living God, whom we are admonished in our text to love with all our minds.

It is really not surprising, once we consider the matter, that in many of our colleges the most rigorous minds in the application of scientific method, whether in the natural sciences or in other studies, are those whose faith in God is thorough and unapologetic. In fact, the work of a scientist takes on a great new seriousness if he is a believer, because then he is not really inventing; he is discovering. The ideas are not

169

merely the puny efforts of his own mind, but represent the thoughts which were before the world was made, and which will be when the world is gone. Every experiment is potentially ennobled by the realization that the scientist is seeking, in his experiment, to ask God a question. The religious scientist has more reason to be careful of his evidence than has the nonreligious scientist, because he is handling what is intrinsically sacred. Shoddiness, for him, is something to spurn because it is a form of blasphemy.

The relationship between the classic faith and modern science may well be one of mutual assistance. At the same time that the faith provides the scientist with a rational groundwork which makes his science part of something bigger than itself, the scientist can help the people of faith by warning them against easy wish-thinking in their belief. Much of the glory of science arises from the steady practice of staying close to what experience teaches and in avoiding mere empty speculation. Science involves some theories, but the final test is always the empirical test. Science can help us all by the insistence that the best reason for believing in the Living God is the scientific reason, viz. that men, representing so many ages and cultures and denominations, have *known Him*. He is not believed in primarily as an inference, but as One who walks with men and women in life's darkest as well as life's brightest ways. He has sustained and He has disturbed. There are millions of humble men, of great intellectual integrity, who belong to the fellowship of verification by the recognition that their lives have been led by God's Hand in theirs. Some may be self-deluded, but not all. If any have not been deluded, God really *is*.

The faith is a thing of wonder, but we dishonor it if we look upon it as an instrument for our use or personal comfort. The faith, when rightly understood, is not our servant, but our master. Find, if you can, a faith in which the urgent question is not what it will do for you, but rather what you can do for it. More important than the ideas you use, are the ideas which use you. Religion, at its deepest, is not so much your search for God as it is God's search for you.

If you have faith in the Living God, and if you hear others speak of it as part of a prescientific view of the universe, and therefore something to be discarded, you can reply with a reasonable answer. You will be telling the truth if you say that it is, at the same time, prescientific, and scientific and post-scientific. It is all these, because it provides the ground of conviction in terms of which science is rationally conceivable, but it is much more than this. It does not burn out as Sputniks do. The faith is an anvil that has worn out many hammers.

THE
POWER
OF SMALL
FELLOWSHIPS

*Where two or three are
gathered in my name, there am I in the midst of them.*
MATTHEW 18:20

There is a sense in which the life of the Christian movement
is ever the same, but there is another sense in which it is
always changing. The faith remains essentially stable
through the generations, but the means by which it is pro-
claimed, expressed, and advanced are bound to be different at
different periods. Once the great orders were new, once Sunday Schools were inaugurated, once foreign missionary work
became organized rather than sporadic. In a similar fashion
new expressions of Christian work and fellowship are emerging in the second half of the twentieth century. Our task is to
understand the novel developments, to thank God for them,
and to profit by them if we can.

Among the most novel features of contemporary Christianity, especially in its Protestant forms, are the small fellowship groups. Though nearly all of the growth of these has
taken place during the few years since the end of the Second
World War, such groups are now numbered by the thousands
in the United States alone, and they are by no means limited
to this country. These groups are usually devoted to prayer,
to study and to discussion, and they seldom include more

172

than ten or twelve persons. Some meet in churches, some in homes, some in offices, some in factories, some in clubs. Ordinarily a group meets once a week for about an hour or perhaps a little more. Some are made up wholly of men, some of women, and some of both sexes, particularly couples. Though there has been some successful development of this kind in the colleges, the great majority who give themselves loyally to this sort of fellowship are men and and women in early middle life.

On the whole, this remarkable development has been essentially spontaneous, in the sense that it has not come to pass as a result of some central organizing agency. Of course people in one community usually hear about groups which meet in other communities and decide that there is nothing to hinder their beginning on their own. A woman's group in a city loses one of its members by removal to another city, and the woman who moves promptly invites the women on her street to join with her in a new prayer group there. This natural method of growth by cell division, according to which division is equivalent to multiplication, led some for a while to speak of the "cell movement," but the term is no longer in common use. Often the groups have no names at all, and many, which have grown up with absolute spontaneity, have no notion that they are matched by hundreds of other groups essentially identical with their own. It is simply a movement whose time has come, and so it comes!

It is not unusual, now, for there to be eight or ten different prayer groups in a single church. There have been as many as nine at one time in Calvary Baptist Church, of Washington, D.C., and there are even more in such churches as the First Presbyterian Church of Fort Wayne or Calvary Episcopal Church in Pittsburgh. It has always been the practice, in the Church of the Saviour, in Washington, for all members to

173

share in groups organized on the basis of intense fellow-ship. Much of the ministry to those outside the membership is performed by the members gathering new people in this way.

Though there is not, and, in the nature of the case, cannot be any standard or orthodox procedure in the meetings of such groups, there is a good deal of similarity in the way in which the meetings are conducted. A common experience is that in which the little group gathers in absolute silence, each one settling down at once to personal, though unspoken, prayer and meditation. Some find that this is facilitated by sitting about an open fire, in a semicircle or on three sides of a hollow square. Usually, several, and sometimes all of those present, break this silence with vocal prayer. Then one member brings up for general consideration either a problem, a special insight, or a passage from the Bible or some other book. The reading is normally most profitable when all have been studying the same book in their homes. Usually the discussion proceeds, for about a half hour, with no person assigned as leader, and then, after a little more spoken or silent prayer, the meeting ends.

The outsider, unfamiliar with this experience, might be pardoned if he were to think it strange that such a meeting could go on, with regularity and with faithful attendance. It seems so simple, so small, so unorganized, so lacking in glamour. Yet, however surprising it may be, such groups show a wonderful tenacity. There are groups, of course, which dissolve so that others can be formed out of the remnants, and there are groups which go utterly to pieces, but the number of those which endure is actually very large. One group of couples, meeting in Toledo, has held together after this fashion for seven years, with marked results in the lives of the members, and, through them, in the life of the community.

So flexible is the method that the composition of the groups

174

can differ widely. Thus, in the Church of the Redeemer in Baltimore, the movement is limited almost wholly to men, particularly business and professional men who have discovered by this means a new understanding of the gospel, with a consequent revolutionary effect upon the church of which they are members. Several are organized in groups called "Dawn Patrols," meeting at 6:30 A.M., chiefly for prayer. They meet at this early hour because they find that it is the one possible time which involves no conflict with any other public responsibility. Many learn that the discipline of early rising, which such meetings require, is a help rather than a hindrance. Other such groups meet at 5:30 P.M., because they learn that the time between the end of the working day and the family dinner is a time of relative freedom or at least can be. Those who stop at bars find it so.

Some meetings succeed in giving to those who are concerned for the Christian cause something of the kind of stern responsibility which Communists feel for the Marxist cause, when they gather in the much publicized Communist cells. Just as each Communist is asked by the day's chairman what he has done for the Communist cause since the last meeting, so the members of the small Christian fellowship are asked to state what they have done for Christ's cause. This is the sort of question which, whether spoken or assumed, tends to make a contemporary small group strikingly different from what most of those present have known before. The usual experience in Christian gatherings has been for there to be inspiration or instruction, but no reporting.

To our shame we have to admit that, though a Communist is, by definition and general understanding, one who is trying to make the Communist cause prevail, there are many "Christians" who accept no such responsibility for *their* cause and are merely doing the expected thing in their community by

175

joining the church. It has not yet occurred to millions of alleged members that they are supposed to engage in specific
tasks which might reasonably be the subjects of report at the
meetings of the faithful.

Usually, in our characteristic Christian gatherings, whether
large or small, all of the talk flows one way, from the plat-
form to the hall, but a contemporary small group breaks this
pattern completely. Many of the changes in lives occur because the participants come to have a wholly new understanding of their responsibilities, when then realize that they are
supposed to be the ones who pray, who advise one another,
who admit their needs, and who plan together some modest
steps in the advancement of Christ's Kingdom.

Often there is a good deal of prayer for specific individuals.
Thus, in an effective prayer group made up of male college
students, someone present will bring up the name of a person
for whom he asks prayer, and all the young men respond
immediately by saying the person's name in unison. Then
they pray silently for him and perhaps some will go on to
pray audibly. Sometimes the problem of someone not present
or even the problem of one of the attenders is presented in
detail. All of this helps to avoid self-centeredness in the praying of the individuals who make up the group.

On the whole, experience shows that in such a group it is
good to introduce, sooner or later, at least three elements,
prayer, study, and discussion. If there is nothing but prayer
the mood runs the risk of being in-grown; if there is nothing
but study it tends to become academic; if there is nothing but
discussion it may become superficial. But the combination
of all three is remarkably fruitful. Most of the groups who
start without study soon decide that they need something
from outside themselves to give them new ideas. The use
of Thomas Kelly's *A Testament of Devotion* or of some

ancient classic has proved valuable as an auxiliary to Bible study.

In one excellent prayer group made up of men, the attenders soon began to find help from the Christian classics and were genuinely surprised by the freshness of the older insights. They wondered why they had to wait for full maturity, to learn even of the existence of some books of exciting worth. One such book which they came to appreciate was *A Serious Call to a Devout and Holy Life* by William Law, an eighteenth-century writer who influenced many in his day, including Dr. Samuel Johnson and John Wesley.

Much as the busy men in the prayer group were helped by the old book by William Law, all agreed that Law was terribly wordy and that many passages were redundant. As a practical consequence the men decided, with the help of their pastor who was also a member of the group, to try to reduce the book to a form in which it would be more profitable to contemporary readers. They worked on the project for about a year and found that they loved it so much that they would try for publication. Now the reduced and substantially improved volume has been published by the Westminster Press and is available to all. This experience tells many lessons at once, including the lesson that people get more out of anything if they take an active part in it. Perhaps other groups will envisage projects of their own, producing materials which they can share with others. This is actually beginning to occur. One group has divided the Gospels and Acts into small manageable sections, each normally devoted to a single topic or story, so that the reader can complete these five books in one year. Now another group has decided to try to do the same for the Epistles and to make their experience generally available. There may be other classics that would profit by reduction; there may be personal prayers which are so helpful that they ought to be shared in print; there are undoubtedly new books that need to be written.

Since we are interested in the entire Christian cause, we need to know how and why these small groups, developed in our time, are as effective and beneficent as they are. In one way the entire idea is highly paradoxical. It is indeed surprising that in a time of unexampled bigness in so many areas of endeavor, the Christian cause should be marked by the conscious production of smallness. While universities and armaments and populations and investments have grown ever more enormous, and while even some churches have become unwieldy in size, many of the most productive of Christian fellowships have been intentionally limited to ten or twelve people.

The reason for the conscious smallness in modern Christian groups is a rediscovery of something very important about human life. What has been rediscovered is that man, who needs fellowship at a deep level almost as much as he needs food, cannot find this except under severely limited conditions. Though it is obvious that the best things do not come by human separateness, it is equally obvious that they do not come in the midst of the crowd. The best things in life come by sharing, and real sharing is impossible under most conditions. The ideal unit for a real meeting of minds and hearts seems to be approximately twelve. If the group is very much smaller the contributions are too slight, while, if the group is very much larger, some begin to feel like the audience, and then the entire idea is ruined. Deep fellowship is a rare and wonderful plant and cannot be grown except under certain circumstances. The intense fellowships of our time have arisen largely because of a new awareness of what the basic unit of Christian fellowship is. It is the same for us that it was for the Apostles.

178

The Church of Jesus Christ is a great and enduring and conquering reality; it is the most important society that we know. But, in spite of its greatness, the church requires, at many points in its history, genuine renewal. And the truly wonderful fact, a fact which verifies its divine origin, is that it is always renewed *on the inside.* We cannot be Christians without the church, for merely individual Christianity is a contradiction in terms, but the church itself goes stale unless there are small redemptive societies which grow up within it to arouse, to stimulate, and to revive. The effect that such societies have on many persons in our generation is truly phenomenal. There are grown men and women who have attended church services for years, without any real lift and without a sense of vitality in their Christian experience, but who finally have been brought into a wholly new kind of life by meeting with a few others in a face-to-face group. Sometimes the new experience has been like a revelation. It is common for thoughtful people to report that, without feeling any reality for years, the love of God is now the dominant thing in their total experience. Many, who have supposedly shared in prayer all of their lives, have suddenly discovered that power of prayer which comes when each person actually prays in a circle where there are none but participators. However hard those who conduct public worship may try to avoid the impression that they are putting on a performance, which others watch somewhat as they watch a play or listen to an orchestra, it is not often that they wholly succeed. Much of the revolutionary effect of small groups arises from the fact that they involve no suggestion whatever of a performance. In them there is participation or there is nothing.

It is important to distinguish between prayer groups which have emerged recently, and the mid-week prayer meeting which was once standard in many Protestant churches. The mid-week prayer meeting still exists in some churches, but in most places it has lost its old vitality chiefly because it is usually nothing more than a pale copy of the Sunday service, with hymns, pastoral prayers, and brief discourses given by appointed leaders in a somewhat informal fashion. There is no similarity between such a service and the meetings of the new fellowships, which often have no leaders at all. The new fellowships must likewise be distinguished from the well-known associations organized about various moral or social causes. For the most part, the new prayer groups refuse to become specific action groups with projects, because the members recognize that there are plenty of service committees already. The great need, they feel, is not for a new pot on the stove, but for new fire under the existing pots.

As the growth of small fellowships continues, we may expect new and creative developments. One such development, which has come as a great surprise to many, is the establishment of a Yokefellow Group in a federal prison. A number of prisoners have built up, since they started in 1955, a really remarkable fellowship of prayer, of study, and of Christian witness. Each alone, as he faces the ridicule of the other prisoners, has a hard time in trying to maintain his conscious Christian discipleship, but the members find that the backing of the other committed ones is of immense help. In a way which those in civil life find difficult to understand, the fellowship of the committed group within prison walls is truly redemptive. Consequently they have much to teach us who are outside. The men have a common predicament, a common penitence, and a common faith which, in their meetings, they share with one another. That their lives are radically changed, both within the prison and after they are paroled, is not surprising. The fact that so much power can emerge in such an unlikely place should stimulate our minds to think of other ways in which the principles of redemptive fellowship can be applied. The probability is that we are still only at the beginning of what may be accomplished in this way; we have hardly scratched the surface. The meaning of "two or three together" is something which is bound to grow in our minds, as we seek humbly to be led along this fruitful path. The wonder is that God has shown us, right in the midst of our troubled time, something that brings freshness to the Christian movement. The power which has emerged in the fellowship of small groups is something which may rightly cause us to thank God and take courage.

THE HOME AS A FORETASTE OF THE KINGDOM

Not for a single day did they cease to teach and preach the gospel of Jesus the Christ, in the temple and at home. ACTS 5:42, Moffatt

There are two societies known to man which serve the redemptive purpose better than any others. One of these is the church and the other is the family. Among the many reasons for the manifest power of early Christianity was the substantial union of these two societies. In the Biblical phrase "the church in the house," the two societies on which we must depend are brought substantially together. Moffatt's translation, at the end of the fifth chapter of Acts, makes the partnership perfectly clear, but rightly reserves the reference to the home as the climax. The disciples, though beaten and warned against further witness, continued, without a break, to spread the message in the temple and at home.

Though we do not usually think of it in this connection, the Christian family is best understood in the light of the entire Christian emphasis on the power of the redemptive group. The philosophy of the family involves not merely biological necessity for human survival, but, far more, the entire Christian philosophy of how redemption takes place. The most common redemptive fellowship is not a prayer group in a church or a factory, but a family in which one man and one

182

woman and children, for whom they are jointly responsible, provide us with the best foretaste of the Kingdom of God that we know on this earth. We are thrilled when we hear of the growth of new prayer groups, but these are as nothing compared to the homes in even a small community. If we count the family units, as we ought, there are millions of redemptive fellowships now in existence.

Each member of the family eventually has his own work to do, his own contribution to make, his own problems to solve, and there is a sense in which each must work alone. Often we wish we could lift the burdens which the others carry; but we cannot do so because they are their burdens, not ours. What helps, however, is the way in which the central fellowship gives each one strength to carry out his particular task in a better and more courageous fashion. *The fellowship gives power, and then the power is used on the periphery after it has been engendered at the center.*

Our hope is that, before it is too late, we may recognize our homes, however modest their arrangement, as places of potential redemption to which people may return from the storm of the world for understanding and strength, and from which they may go out to do the work the world so sorely needs to have done. Thus life takes on a beautiful rhythm. We go into the fellowship for renewal and go out from it for service in the world. Health depends upon the continual vibration or alternation, similar to that of the motion of lungs and heart. People who would serve adequately in the world must find redemptive centers in which, no matter how great their frustrations and disappointments, they become new people.

It is only because we are so familiar with it that the Christian family fails to fill us with wonder. We take it for granted that each should do all he can for the others without counting the cost, but this is really marvelous. Even very poor homes are often scenes of such affection and concern that there is a complete refusal to limit personal liability for one another. The family, when rightly understood, is not an organization in which there is a carefully delineated division of labor, though there may be accepted distinctions among duties, but rather one in which each will do for the others all that he can. The child is not kept from having the shoes she needs merely because she has not earned them; the mother may work far harder than any of the children, yet receive less than any of them in the division of family expenditures. This contrast is particularly striking when a child is handicapped. The family unit is marked, then, not by careful bookkeeping, with a strict balance between labors and rewards, but by an almost divine unconcern for such considerations. The sacredness of the family lies in the fact that the basis of union is that of uncalculating affection.

Of course this family ideal is often missed or actually rejected in practice. What is worth while, however, is the constant effort to state the standard in such a clear way that we at least know when we have missed it. As long as the conception is clear, we have a check upon our failures and an incentive to recovery of the ideal in practice. It is because the family ideal is so advanced and so elevated that failure in achieving it is obviously tragic. It is not tragedy for a man to give up membership in a lodge or even in a particular church; but divorce, even when justified, is always a tragedy.

Though we make much, as we ought, of the danger of deep rifts between husband and wife, partly because they become matters of public information when divorce proceedings are undertaken, we do not seem to be equally aware of the danger of deep rifts between parents and children. Sometimes the tension between the generations is far more damaging than is the tension within the same generation. Frequently the father is extremely critical of what his sons and daughters do, contrasting their actions with his own at the same age, while the young people think that their parents are hopeless back numbers. This problem can never be entirely eliminated, so long as we have different generations, but there is an approach to it which includes real hope. This is the religious approach in which, in the experience of prayer, whether public or private, all recognize their own weaknesses and needs. Insofar as the family is seriously trying to be a small redemptive society, the main dangers of hatred are largely overcome in advance. There are problems which cannot normally be solved on a purely secular level, but which are highly soluble on the deeply religious level. There is no area of experience in which this is more true than that of family life.

We have often heard the proverb that charity begins at home; but, if the foregoing conception of a redemptive society is correct, Christianity also begins at home. The chief way in which the world is changed and made to resemble more accurately the Kingdom of God is by the effect of an increasing number of small societies in which this Kingdom is already partly demonstrated. It is not that we develop our Christian gospel in public life and then, as a result, apply it to our domestic situation, but rather that the home is really its seedbed. Here the new life normally starts, and from here it can be transplanted. The enemies of the gospel would not be disturbed by full churches if only they could eliminate Christianity from the homes.

It is really very wonderful that modest people like ourselves can share in anything as powerful and as uncalculating as unmercenary love. There is a sense, of course, in which this is part of our natural human behavior; but that is not the whole story. The rest of the story is that there is something about the Christian gospel which has deepened and tightened

185

the family bond. Very early it was recognized that the gospel was incompatible with the exposure of infants and the relegation of wives to a secondary status. Though the family has promoted the gospel, the gospel has, at the same time, ennobled the family. The entire process, by which this has been accomplished, began by the decision of Christ to use the term Father, which arises from family experience, as the least inadequate term by which to designate the Maker and Sustainer of the universe. The best language of religion emerges from the language of the home.

The chief practical glory of this philosophy is that it gives all who live in families, and this is most people, the realization that they can be engaged in extending Christ's Kingdom. Each mother who cares unselfishly for her children, both materially and spiritually, is a participant in a genuine ministry. She is helping to produce one of the many tiny societies without which the world would sink into rapid decay. It is the home that sends young people to college; it is the home that sends men into factories; it is the home that sends people to church.

It is not given to us to know exactly how and when the Kingdom will come. Some believe it will come finally in a great single burst, and they could be right. Indeed, there are some of Christ's expressions which seem to point this way; but there are other expressions which indicate that the Kingdom will come by the infection of small redemptive centers. This would seem to be the chief point of the parables of the mustard seed and the leaven which appear together in the gospel.

The individual home, with its beds and games and dining table and books, may seem a tiny thing in contrast to states and governments and armies; but it is by means of such tiny things that the world is changed. The home may, like the mustard seed, be the least of all seeds; but seed it undoubtedly is. If we could have enough really good homes, we should have a very different world; and we are not likely to have a good world without them.

The good homes do not come by accident. It is undoubtedly true that there are good homes, marked by deep and enduring affection, in which there is no conscious Christian emphasis at all, but there is greater likelihood of success in these matters if there is a uniting faith at the center. Ordinarily we love each other better if we love God first. The best affection comes as a by-product when noble things are attempted and done together. "Life has taught us," wrote Exupéry, "that love does not consist in gazing at each other, but in looking outward together in the same direction."

The late Dr. Henry T. Hodgkin helped many of us by his comparison of the home to an island. He pointed out in *The Christian Revolution* that our modern continents emerged originally from the sea as separated islands, which were really the tops of mountains. The continents grew by the increase in the number of these islands. Each home, Dr. Hodgkin believed, can be a small island which is a truly manageable unit. We cannot change the whole world at once; we cannot alter greatly a political party or a labor union, or even a local church; each of these is too much for us. But, in the little island which we call home, we can set the conditions to a remarkable degree. This is where each is able to make a radical difference. This is how the world can be changed.

Every young woman who is a wife and mother, often with tasks far beyond her meager strength, can take great satisfaction in this idea. There is one little realm where she can be as a queen. She may not always succeed, but the truth is that there is nowhere, in all the world, any point at which we succeed better. The holy task of managing this little kingdom, as

187

an island of peace in a sea of confusion, is one which requires all of the intelligence, all of the devotion, and all of the education which anyone is ever likely to have. Even at best, parents are not wise enough, because the intellectual decisions involved in the mental and moral guidance of children are so difficult. God, even in His mercy, never gave any one parent enough brains.

Though we all understand that both father and mother have heavy responsibilities in the guidance of a home, there is a sense in which the mother has and ought to have the major task. She is normally closer to it. It is by the success of her home, more than by any other means, that her life will be given true dignity and meaning. The system set up by Lenin would rob the woman of this, by making her just as much a wage earner as the father, and with no more responsibility for the home. Our danger, in the life of the West, is that we shall move in the same direction, not because of a conscious Communist philosophy, but simply by default or because of ever-increasing material desires. This is one of the places in which a deliberately held Christian philosophy can make a practical difference.

A serious difficulty in the system according to which both parents are fully employed outside the home, while the state takes over the care of the children, is that the home inevitably fails in its teaching function. That the good home must be a place of teaching, however, is increasingly clear. This is particularly true in regard to religious education. Where will the love of God be inculcated if not in the home? We may wish it could be done in our public schools, but, in practice, this is really impossible. However deeply we deplore it, we know very well that the introduction of any specific religious teaching into the tax-supported schools would carry with it the serious danger of sectarian emphasis. No matter how much she tries to avoid it, the teacher is almost sure to slant her religious instruction toward the view of her own denomination. This is part of the price we pay for living in a mixed society.

The only other alternative is the Sunday School or the weekday religious instruction on released time or after school hours. We want all of this that we can get, and we want it to be handled as well as possible, but we know that it does not and cannot meet the full need. Though some of this public instruction is excellent, much of it is poor and fragmentary. Moreover, there are millions of children who are not involved in it at all. Consequently there is no satisfactory solution of the problem which does not involve the mother as the teacher of faith. If we understand this, and if we really believe it, we shall use some of our time and energy to teach mothers to teach religion more intelligently in their homes. This ought to be one of the chief functions of a church.

Even when the Christian faith is well taught in churches, it must be supplemented in homes. This can be done by parents working alone or in groups. Some of the most promising of contemporary experiments are devoted to domestic group teaching, thus producing the church that is in the house. This identification of the home and the faith involves a great psychological advantage. There is always a danger that children will think of religion as something confined to a special building with a special kind of architecture, and appropriate only for special days. Much of this danger is avoided if the study of the Bible or of Christian history is conducted on a weekday in an ordinary house which is a center of living and loving and working. The church building and the domestic building need not be rivals for the affectionate interest of the young, but can serve complementary purposes.

We need to use all of the imagination we can muster to

think how to make prayer, which is the heart of true religion, real in our homes. Certainly we want to avoid the mistake of allowing it to seem burdensome or forbidding, with the sad consequence that independent young minds rebel. If we are to avoid this outcome it is necessary to keep our religion gay and as natural as eating or sleeping. No doubt the very best practice is to see to it that every meal, in which the whole family participates, begins with a time of reverence. Here variety, within the general pattern, is a help. Sometimes we should sing, sometimes we should pray in silence, sometimes there should be the use of classic prayers, sometimes there should be spontaneous prayers on the part of members of different ages. Above all we should not be selfconscious about praying in the presence of one another. We are failing if we cannot make the experience of thanking God as natural and as wholesome as the experience of telling one an other of our love and admiration. When we recognize the incredible compliment that God has paid us in allowing us to influence, in such measure, the lives of growing human beings, prayer is the only normal response. All of the major occasions in family life, whether birthdays or anniversaries or starting to school or marriage, are of such intrinsic importance that they become occasions for prayer whenever the Christian religion is taken seriously. Pleasance Gurney has shown us the way in which family occasions can be glorified, especially in her prayer for the Anniversary of Wedding Day:

We kneel today before Thee, Lord, and thank Thee for another year of our lives spent together. We are grateful for Thy love and goodness to us and we pray that the coming year of our married life may bind us more closely to each other. May we bravely and courageously face all that comes and with wisdom and encouragement help each other along the road of life, ever rejoicing in the gift of mutual love which Thou hast given us. Amen.

190

Few families in modern times have demonstrated more perfectly the conception of the home as a Christian society than that of Samuel and Susanna Wesley at Epworth. Today, because the Old Rectory has been restored and dedicated to a new public purpose, it is relatively easy for us to reconstruct in imagination the life that went on there two hundred and fifty years ago. Since their part of Lincolnshire was really an island, cut off from its surrounding territory much of every year, the cultural isolation of Epworth was extreme. Consequently, the Wesley family had to make the most of its own resources. Susanna reigned as the queen of her little kingdom in a way that has become a wonder to the world. Every day was filled with careful teaching, with laughter, with work, and with prayer. The powerful life developed in this small sphere has now touched the lives of millions through the ministry of Susanna's sons John and Charles. Though they started in isolation, the world became their parish. Here is an almost perfect illustration of how the Christian life proceeds. It is cultivated in small centers of affectionate concern, and from these centers redemptive influences radiate. The glory of the pattern is that it is by no means limited to the rich and powerful, but can be followed by people in all kinds of circumstances. It is practical because it is potentially universal.

The philosophy involved in this conception of how the world is changed is akin to that of Howard Thurman's emphasis on the "growing edge." Those who observe the desert are well aware of the way in which the relatively inconspicuous oasis begins to conquer the wasteland. A single blade of grass, alone in the desert, would be sure to wither and die, while seed sown indiscriminately would almost certainly be wasted, but the little oasis often wins by growing at its edges. This it does by making its own soil as it slowly advances, the life of the growing edge being sustained by the background support of the other life immediately behind it. Even this process does not always win, because sometimes the desert overwhelms the little spot of greenness, but no other known method has any real prospect of success. This is the philosophy inherent in the Christian gospel of the Kingdom. It is by the many little kingdoms that the world is changed. These little kingdoms may be of various kinds, but the very best example known to us is the redemptive society which is called a home.